# East End Photos
## Through Mayar's Eyes
Photo Album: Tower Hamlets, Random, Two

### Mayar Akash

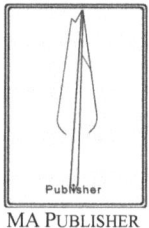

MA PUBLISHER

Copyright © Mayar Akash 2020

Published by MA Publishing (Penzance)
Published October 2020
ISBN-13: 978-1-910499-60-3

All rights reserved. No part of this publication may be reproduced, stored in a retrieval system, or transmitted, in any form or by any means, electronic, mechanical, photocopying, recording, public performances or otherwise, without prior written permission of the copyright holder, except for brief quotations embodied in critical articles or reviews.

Cover designed by Mayar Akash
Typeset in Times New Roman
All photos belong to Mayar Akash

Paper printed on is FSC Certified, lead free, acid free, buffered paper made from wood-based pulp. Our paper meets the ISO 9706 standard for permanent paper. As such, paper will last several hundred years when stored.

# Introduction

This is 3rd photo books of the series, 2nd of the Tower Hamlets random two featuring the photographs I've taken over the years growing up in the East End of London. When I first got my first camera in the late 80's, as I grew and my curiosity and ideas changed and formed and I started snapping away where my tenacity drew me. Today I present those photos captured through My Eyes, The environment changed along with the people and social issues, they all had a bearing on my world.

For many years I didn't know what to do with them but now it seem fit to organise them like an albums and publish them, give access to the world, to see the East End through a Bangladeshi, Sylheti living in Tower Hamlets, with the urban factor; no hold bars assimilation into the Cockney East End, perspective.

The photos are not in any particular order, they are all random, I want to give people a taster of random things that I have encounter in my life journey.

I have ensured that all images as clearly marked with the date and the time stamp, and for some images brief description to assist, however, generally just date and time. The images are random and peruser's interpretations will be subjective, and that is how I feel is best left.

"Date & Time stamped photos, I know where I was, do you know where you were in the world?"

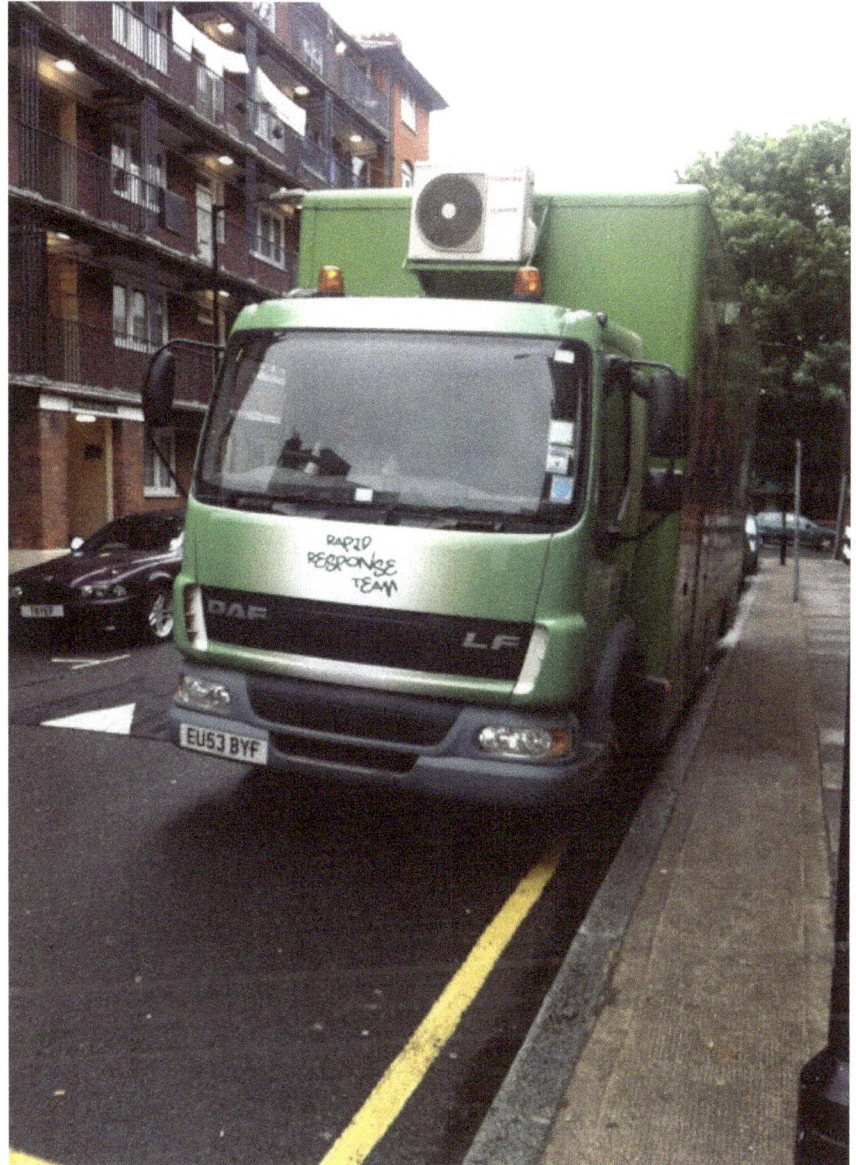

29.5.2013 - 18:04:52, RRT BUS, Shadwell

Different Coloured buses were equipped with different facilities and went to differed parts of the borough.

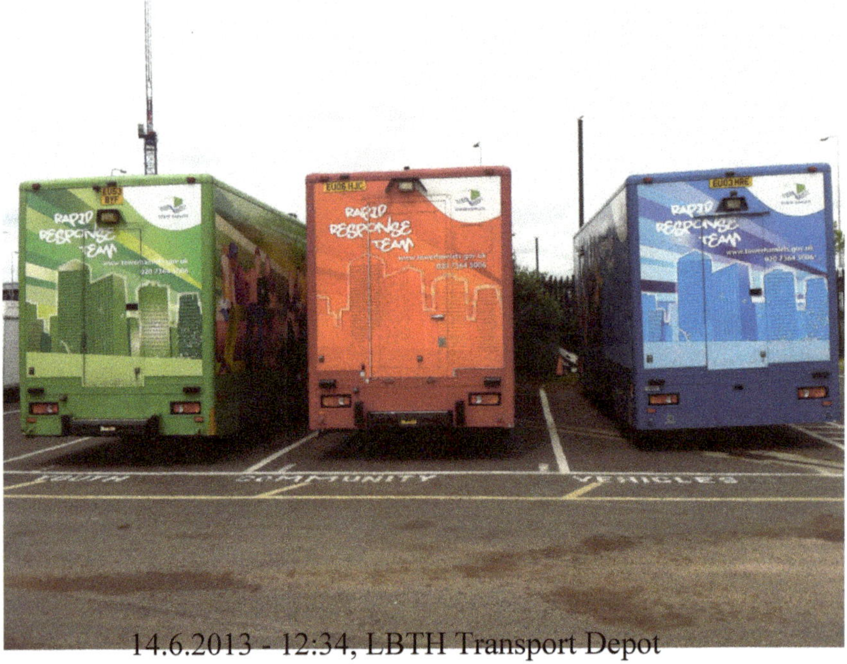

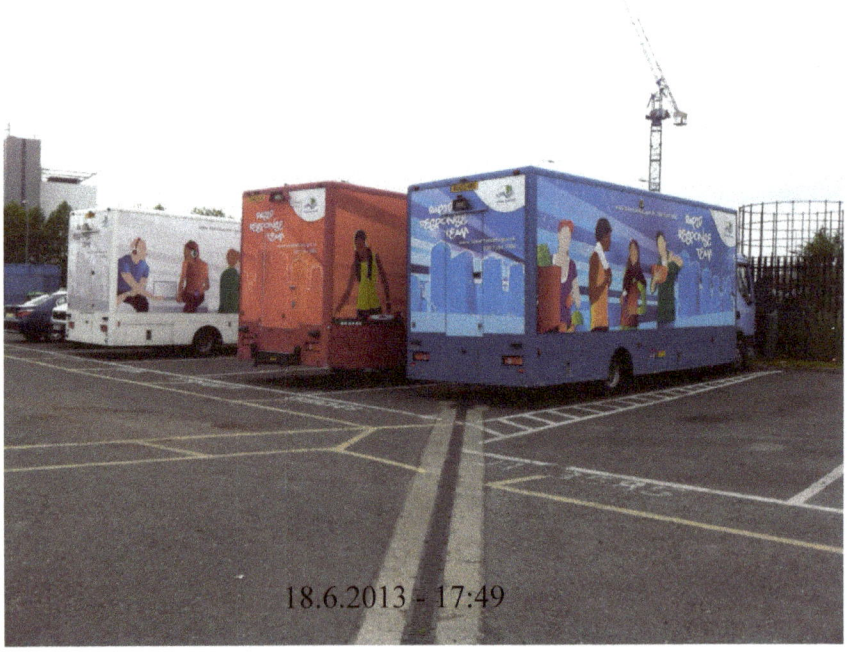

14.6.2013 - 12:34, LBTH Transport Depot

18.6.2013 - 17:49

East End Photos, Through Mayar's Eyes : **Tower Hamlets, Random One**

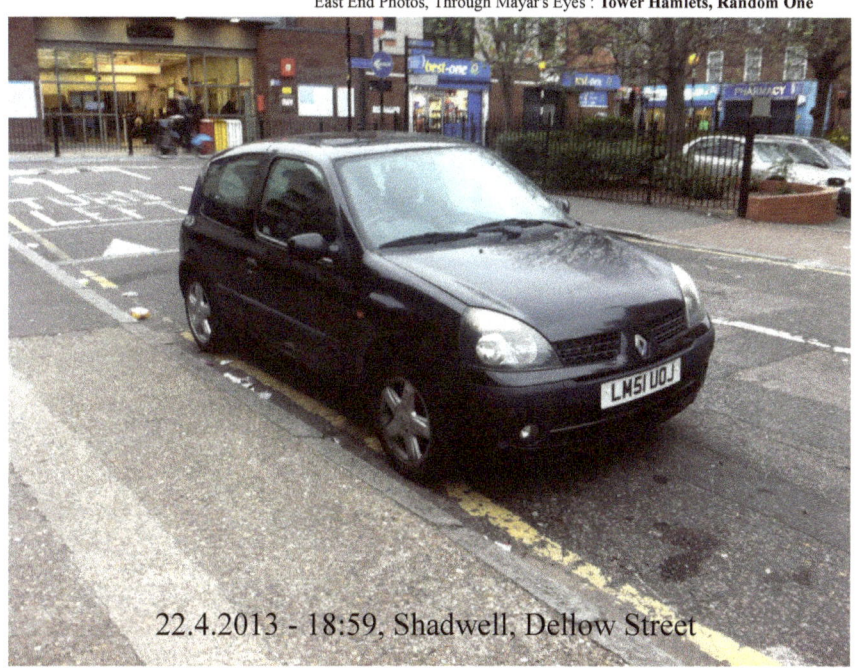

22.4.2013 - 18:59, Shadwell, Dellow Street

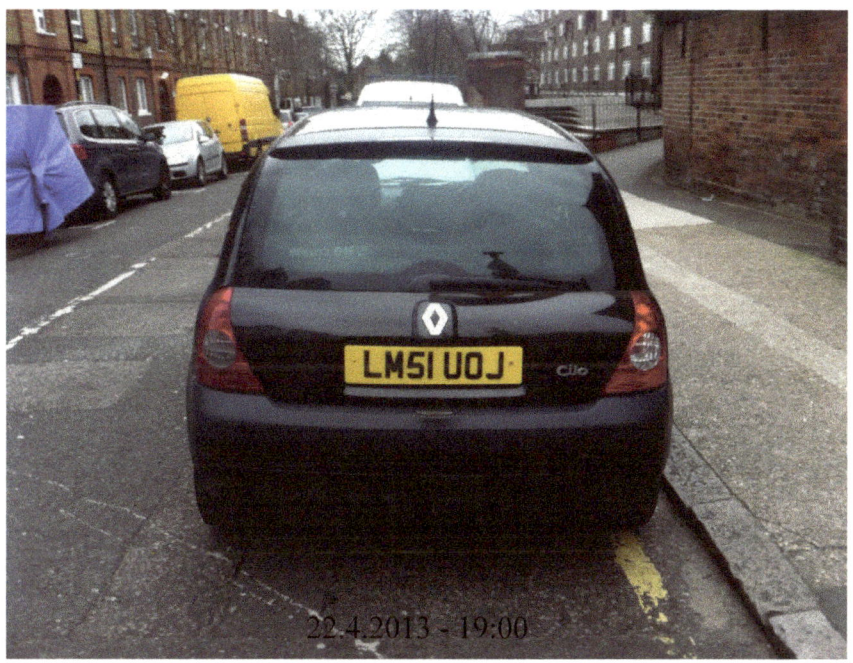

22.4.2013 - 19:00

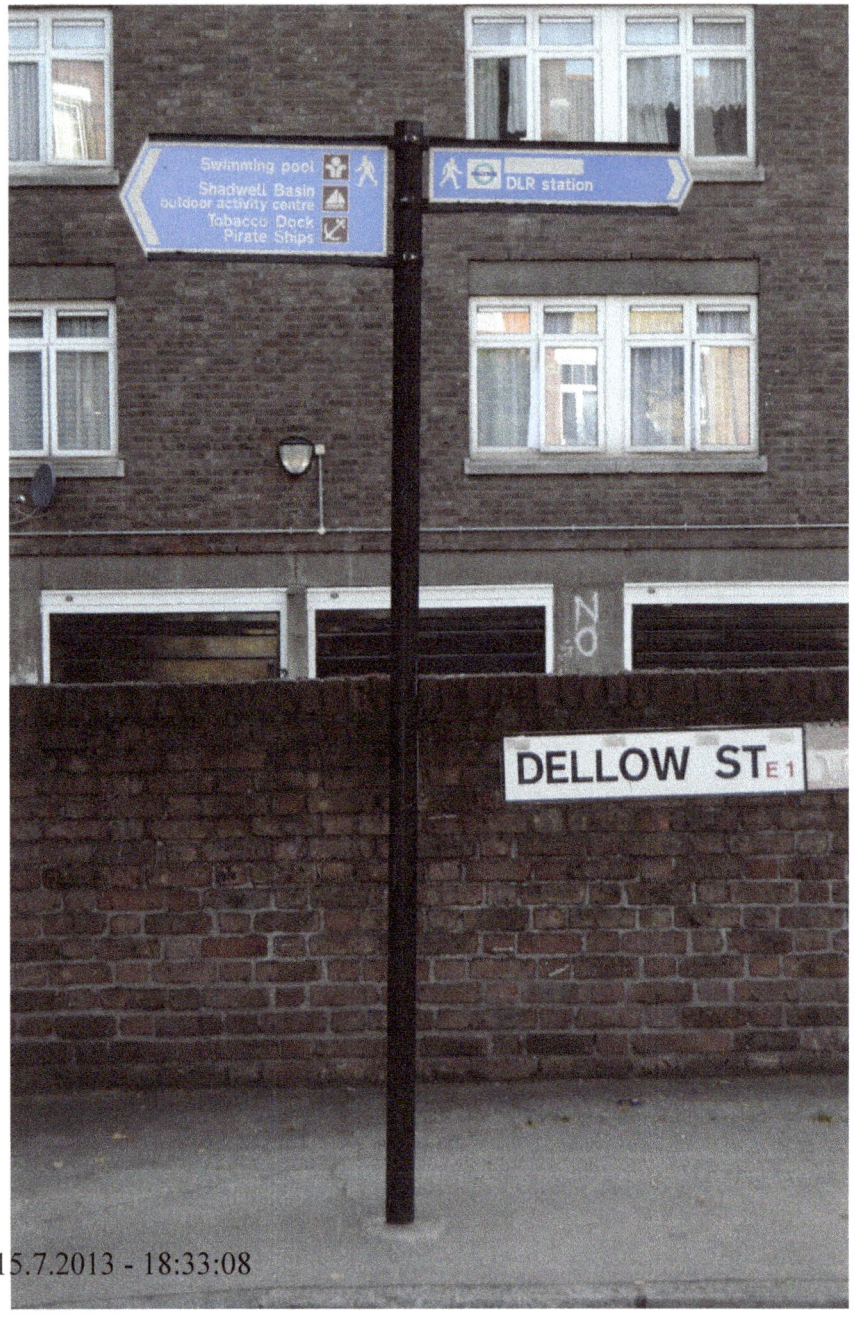

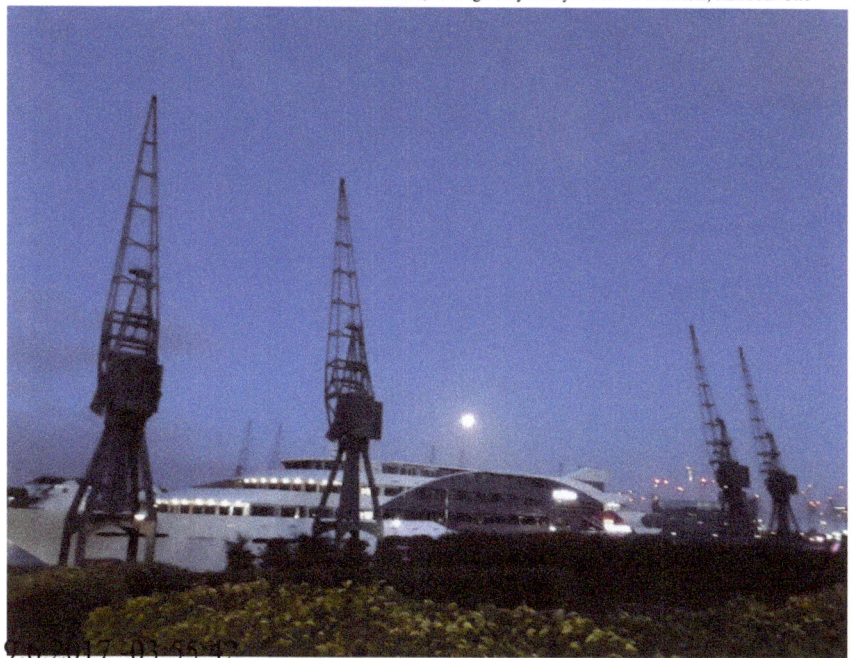

9.6.2017 - 03:55:42, Silvertown, Excell Centre

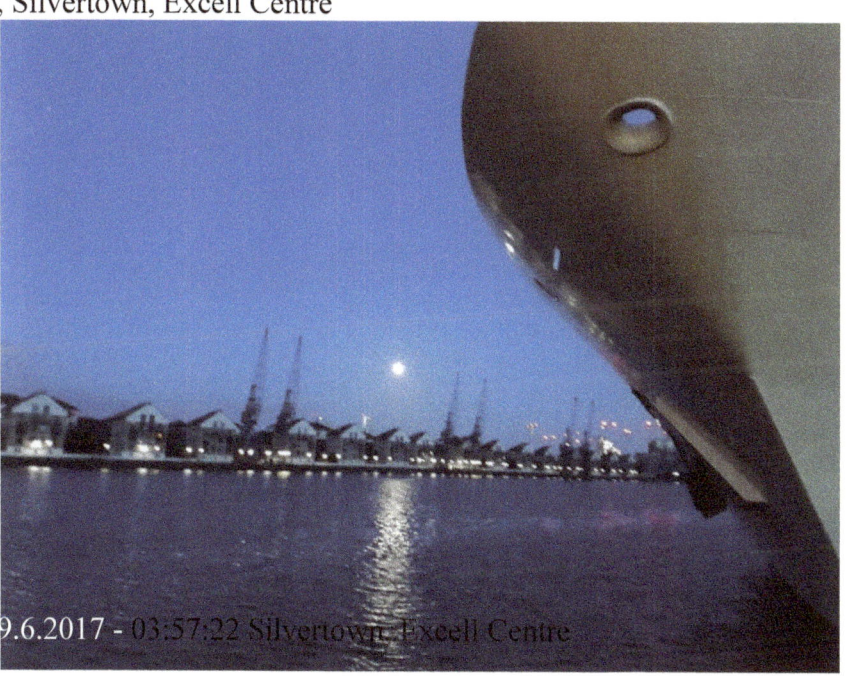

9.6.2017 - 03:57:22 Silvertown, Excell Centre

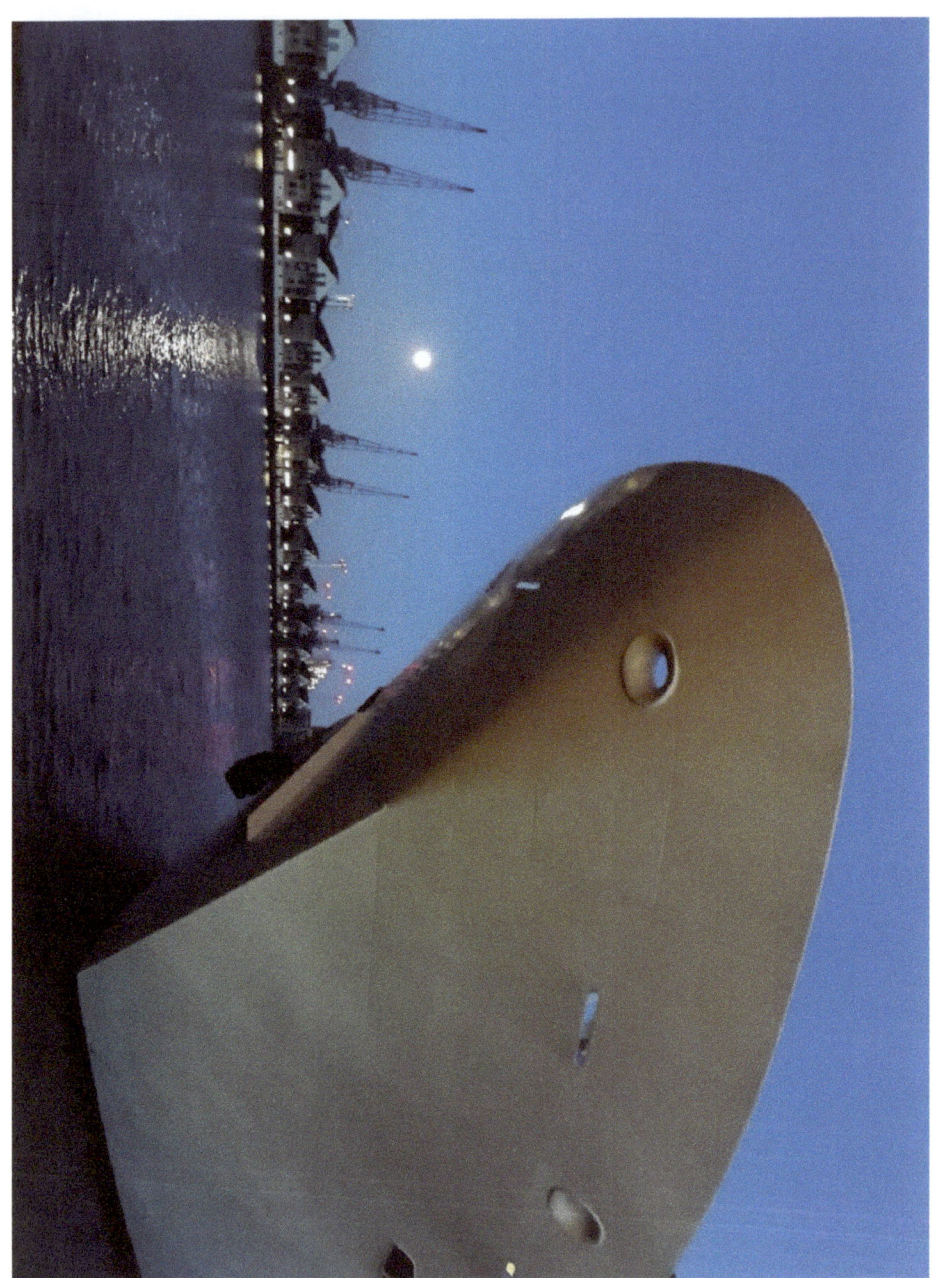

9.6.2017 - 03:58:05

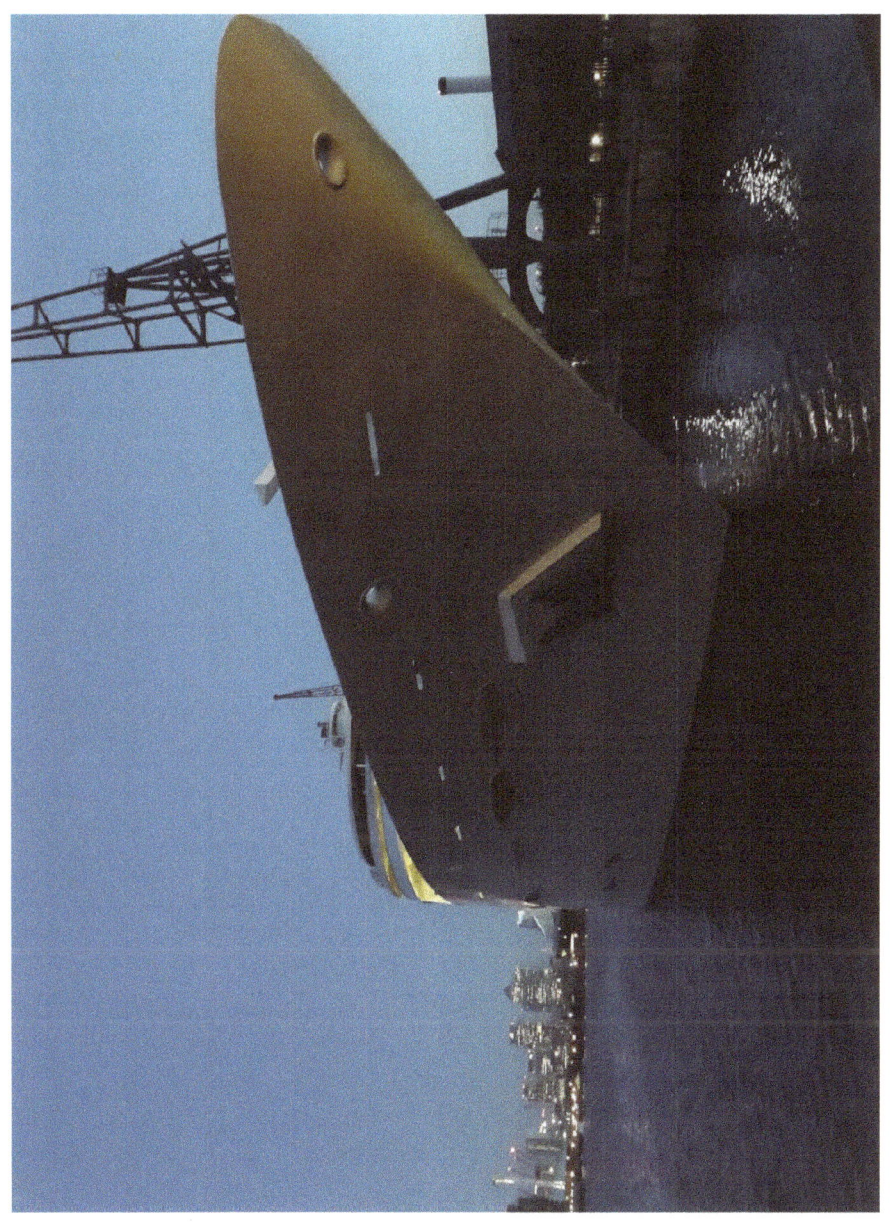

9.6.2017 - 03:58:44

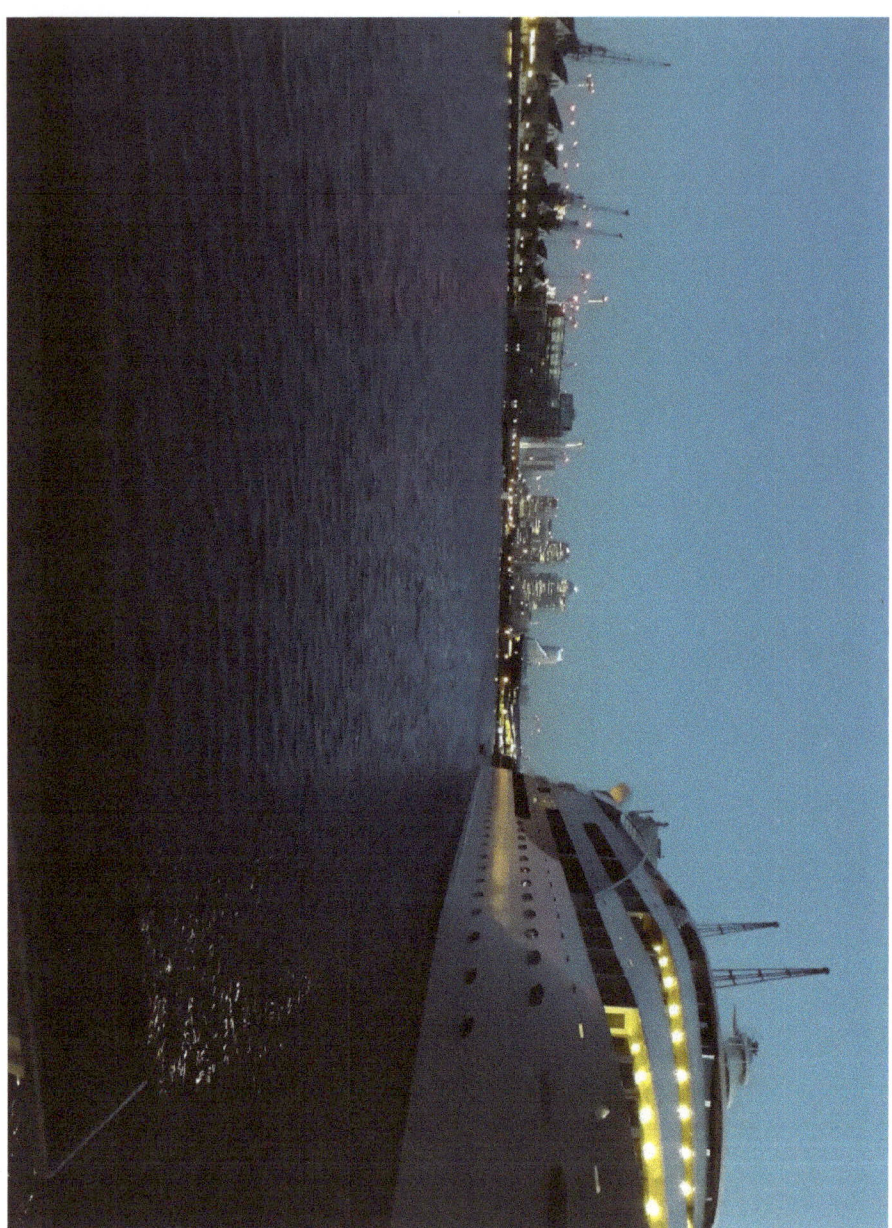

9.6.2017 - 03:59:35

East End Photos, Through Mayar's Eyes : **Tower Hamlets, Random One**

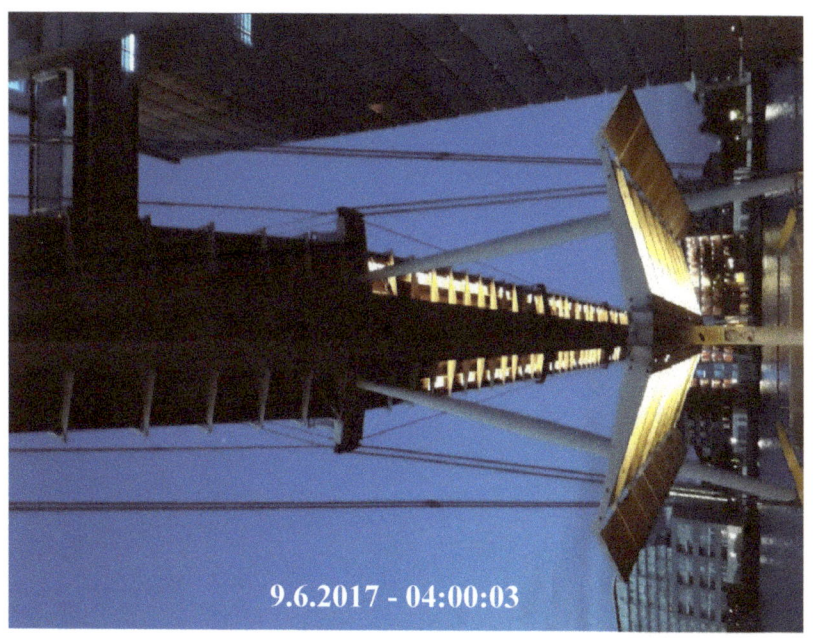

9.6.2017 - 04:00:03

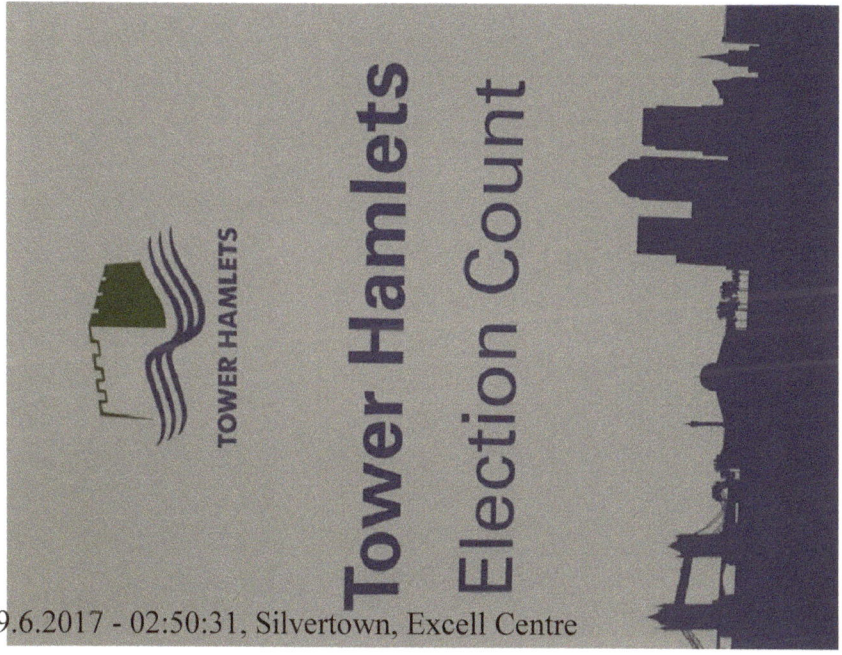

9.6.2017 - 02:50:31, Silvertown, Excell Centre

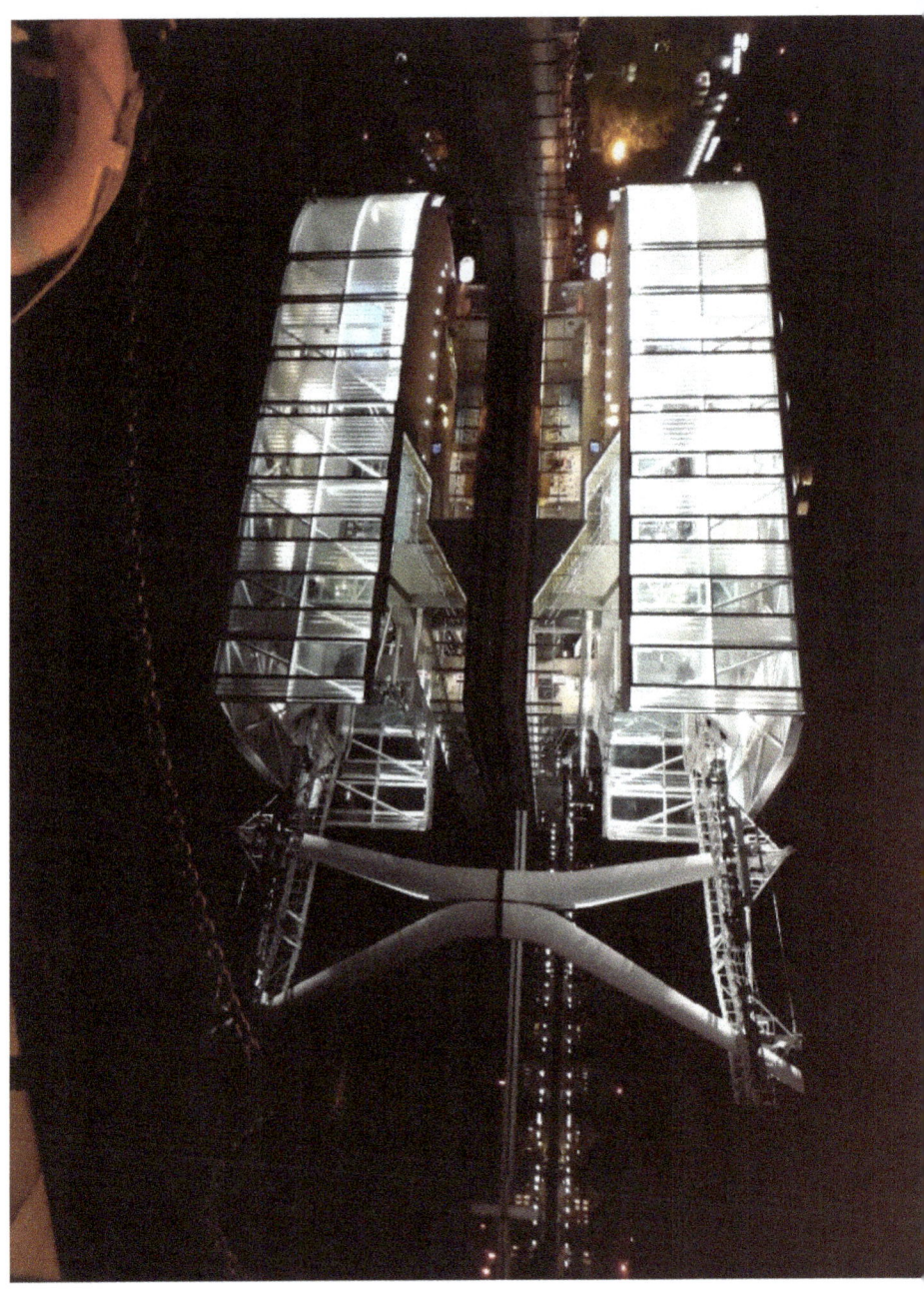

17.10.2017 - 21:39:36, Silvertown

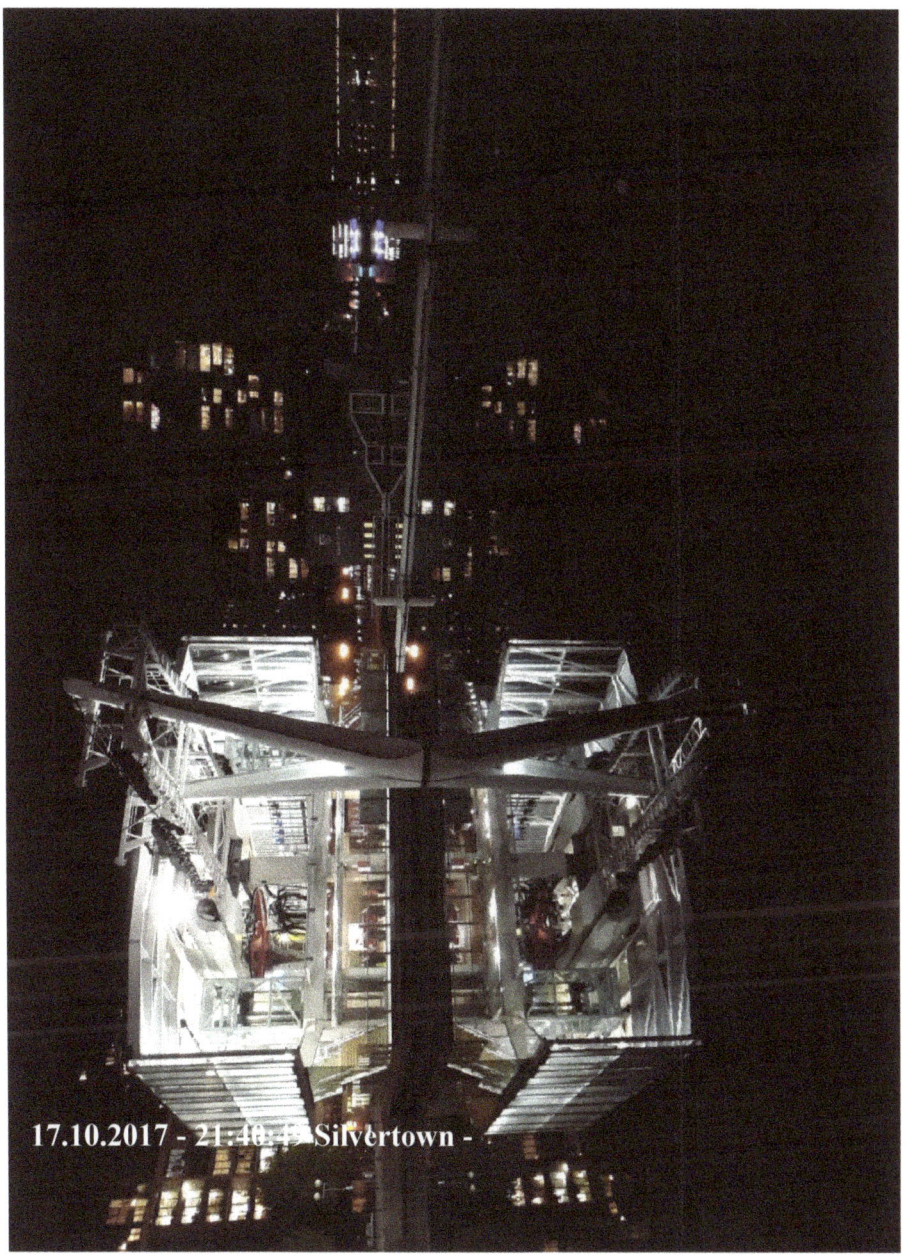

17.10.2017 - 21:40:15 Silvertown -

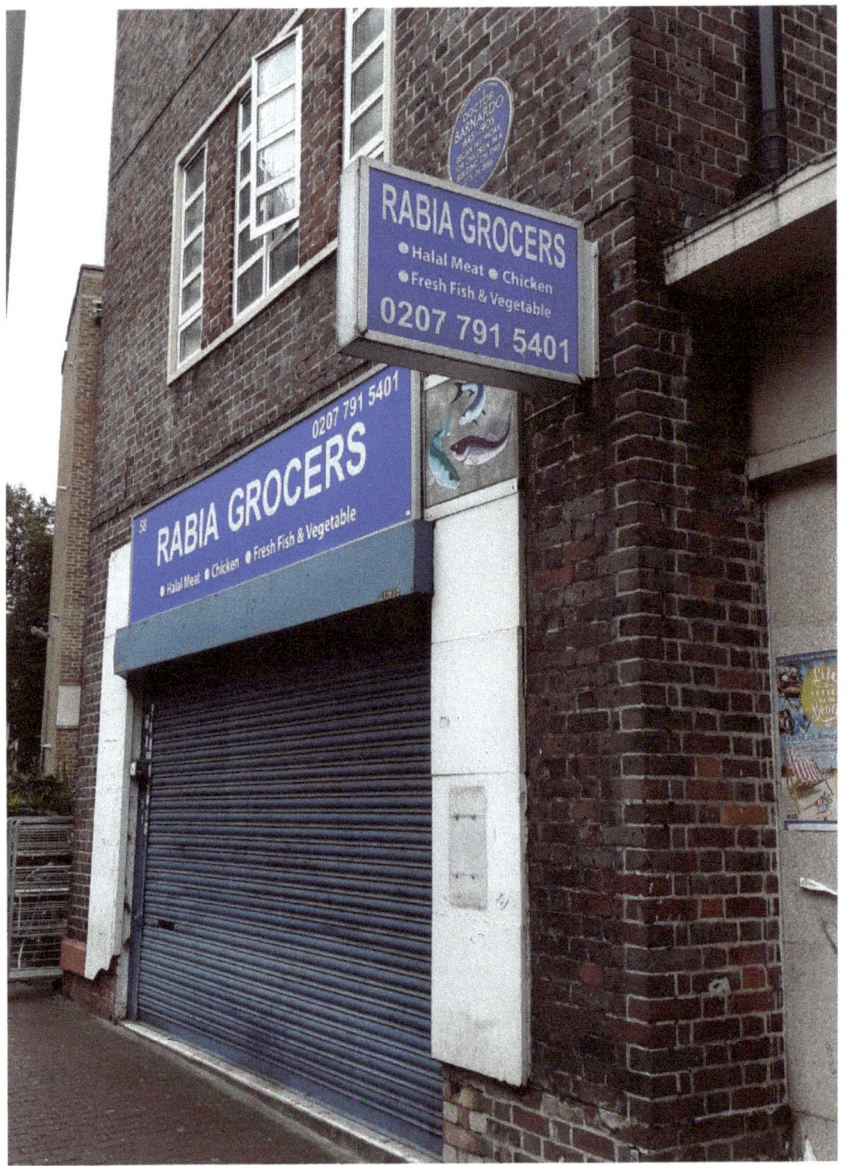

18.10.2017 - 12:18:00, Ben Johnson Road, Shopping square

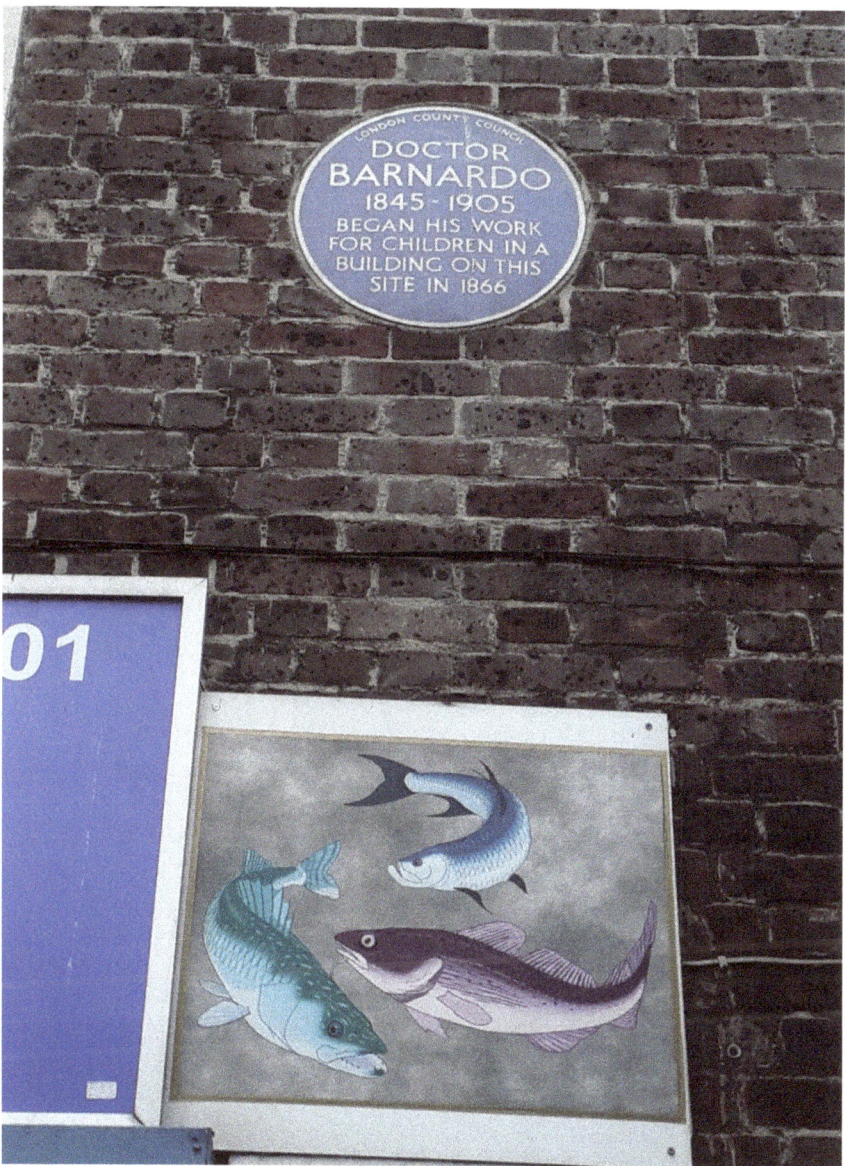

18.10.2017 - 12:28:15

Mayar Akash

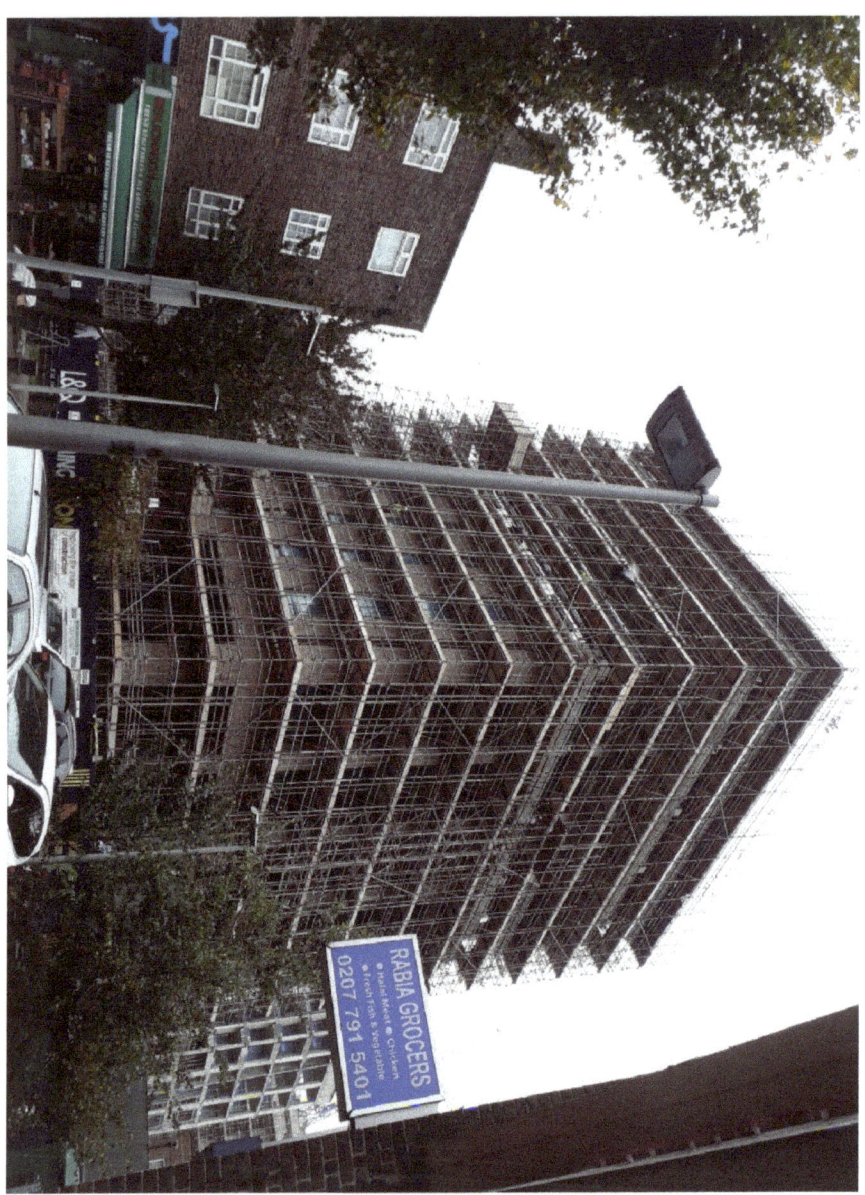

18.10.2017 - 12:29:55

**KITCAT TERRACE, ST MARYS CHURCH HALL, E3 2SA**

| Mukith | 1134 |
|---|---|
| Abzal Ali | 4383 |
| Ahmed Mire | 3144 |
| Aisha Ali | 5054 |
| Akhtar Rahim | 5995 |
| Corrine Ffinch | 3634 |
| Edwin Lewis | 0475 |
| Gelu Miah | 5991 |
| Holly Samed | 4715 |
| Imran Khan | 3377 |
| Joynul Ahmed | 1612 |
| Kay Mala | 0405 |
| Lipe Begum | 5053 |
| Mavis Sekyi | 2058 |
| Mayar Akash | 3292 |
| Michelle Williams | 4319 |
| Momota Hussain | 5834 |
| Mostak Ahmed | 3154 |
| Rena Begum | 4865 |
| Saddique Ahmed | 5970 |
| Sadique Miah | 5719 |
| Sajjad Chowdhury | 0637 |
| Samantha Anderson | 0953 |
| Steve Weeks | 0903 |
| Toahel Mohammed | 5515 |
| Yasin Abdi | 1315 |
| Zamida Begum | 5780 |
| Targeted Youth Support Fax No. | 2418 |
| **TYS DUTY** | 2707 |

13.6.2017 - 11:41:09

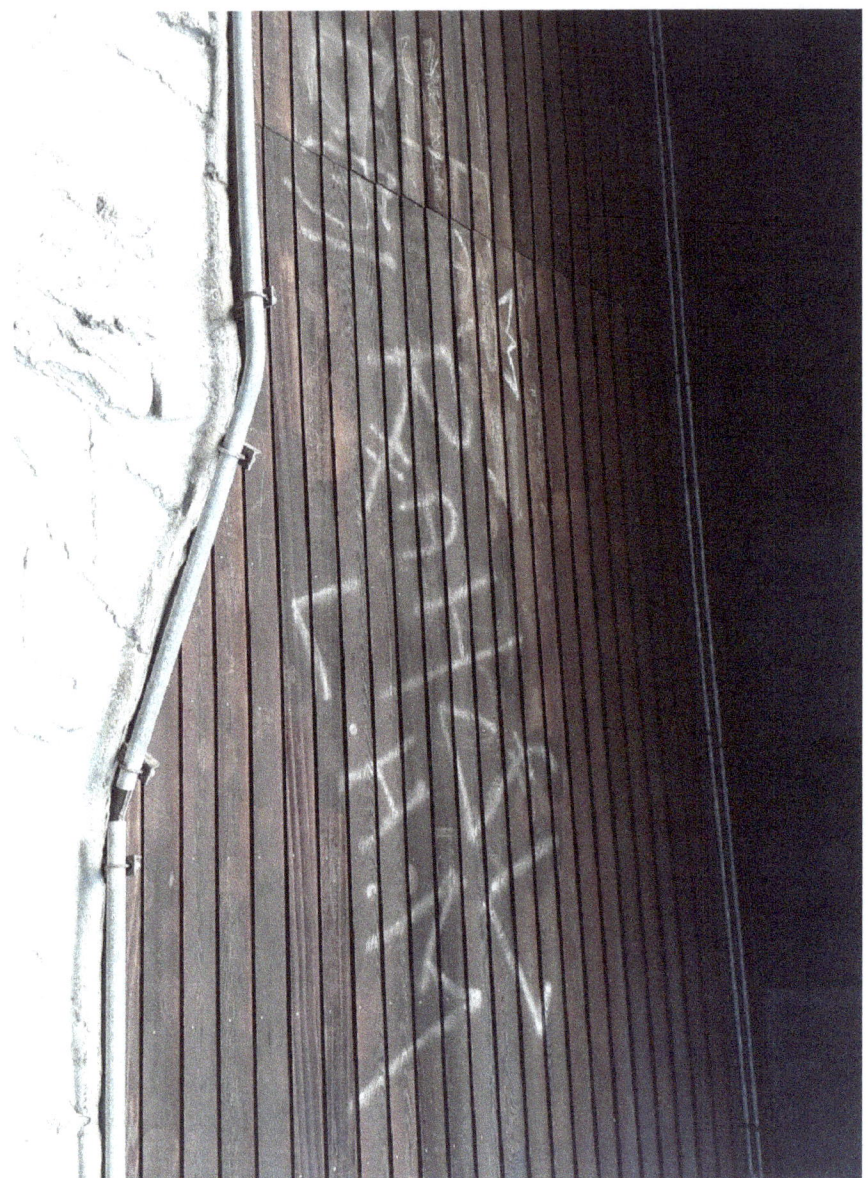

30.10.2017 - 14:34:20, LimeHouse Youth Centre

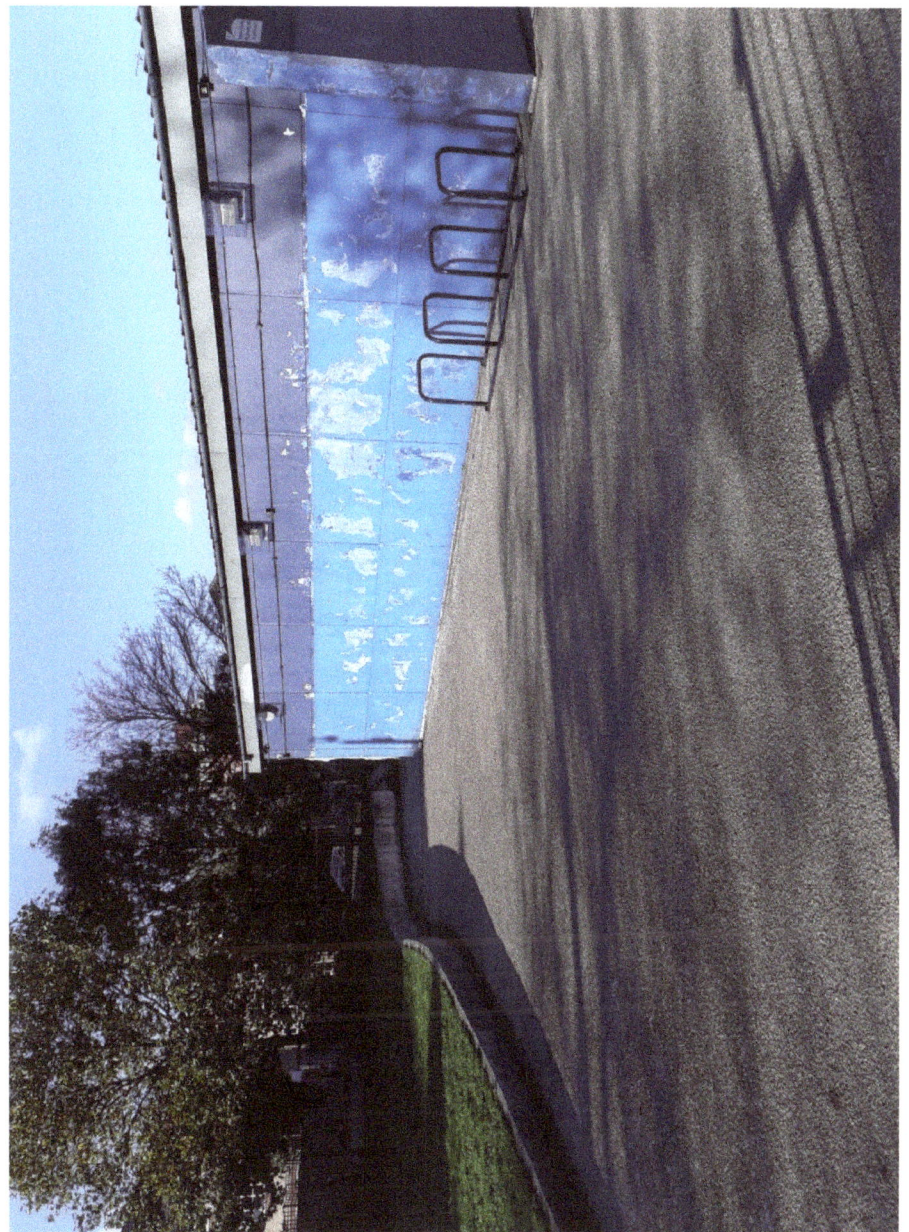

6.11.2017 - 13:40:31, Isle of Dogs, Youth Centre

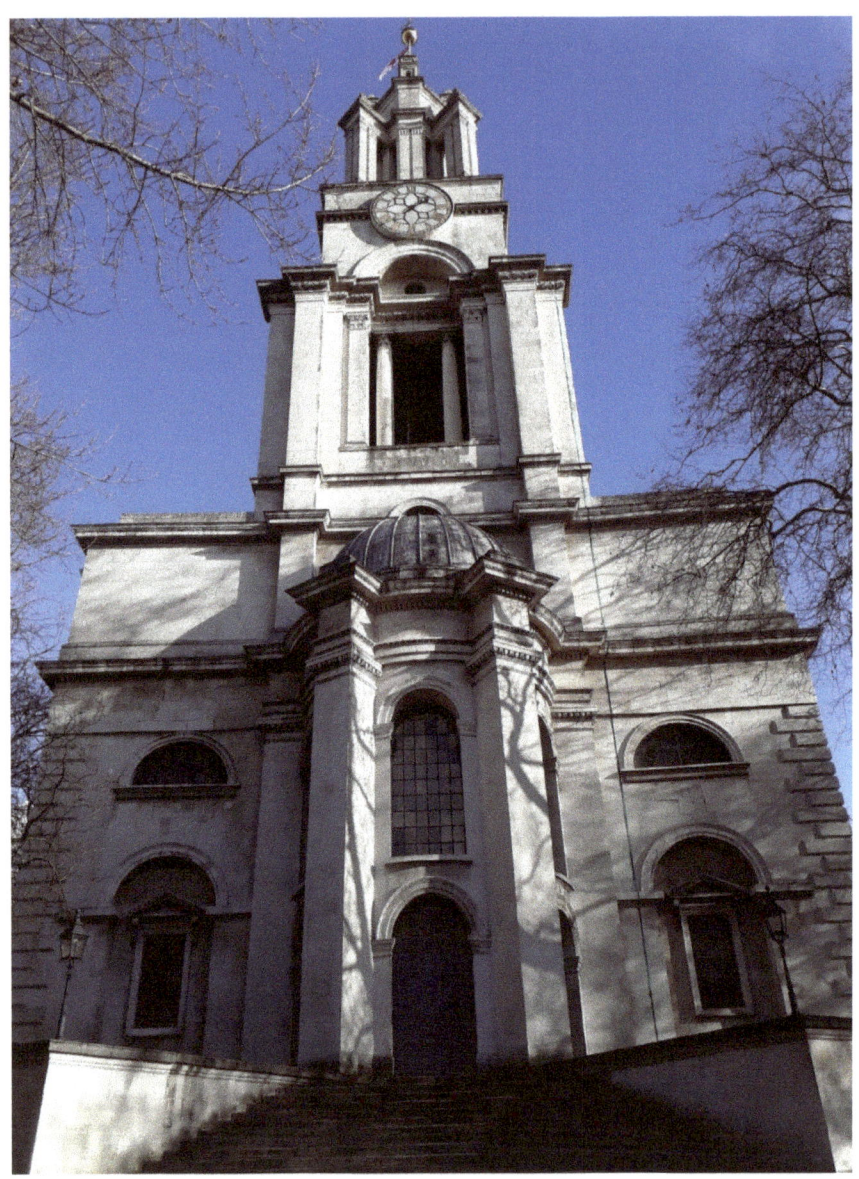

25.01.2018 - 13:35:38

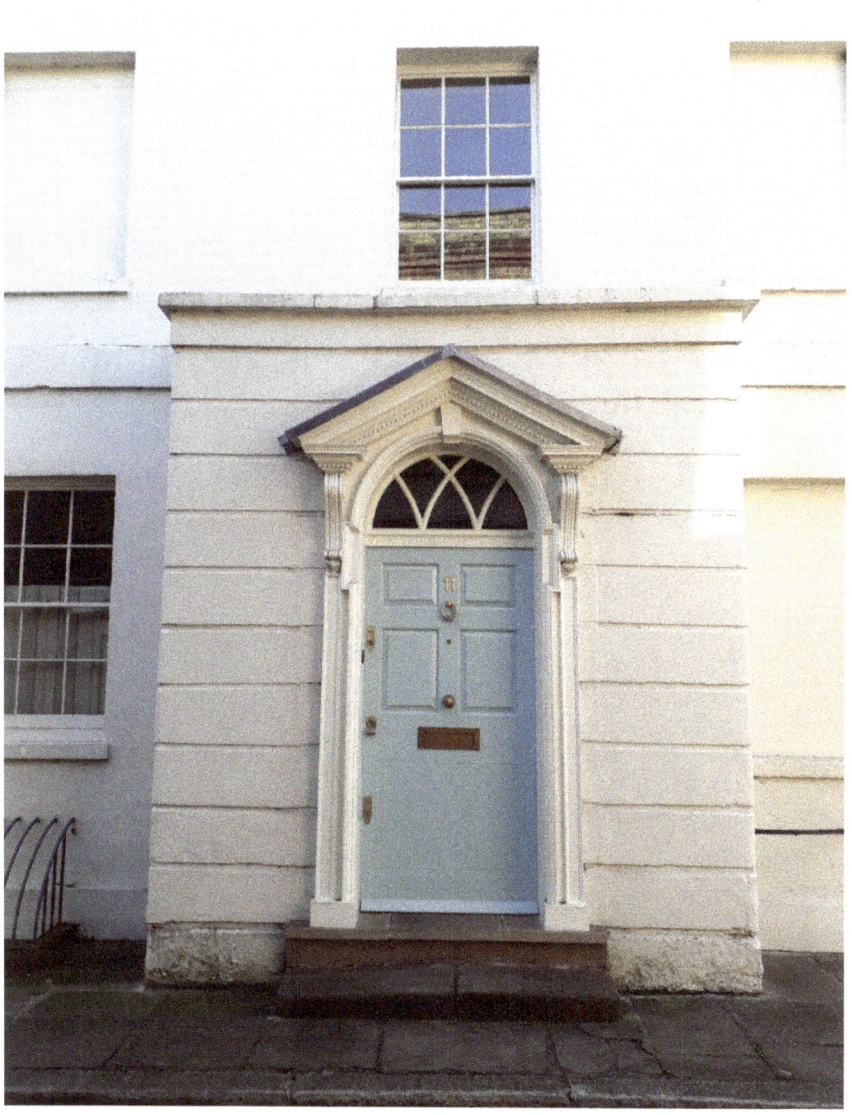

**25.01.2018 - 13:36:20**

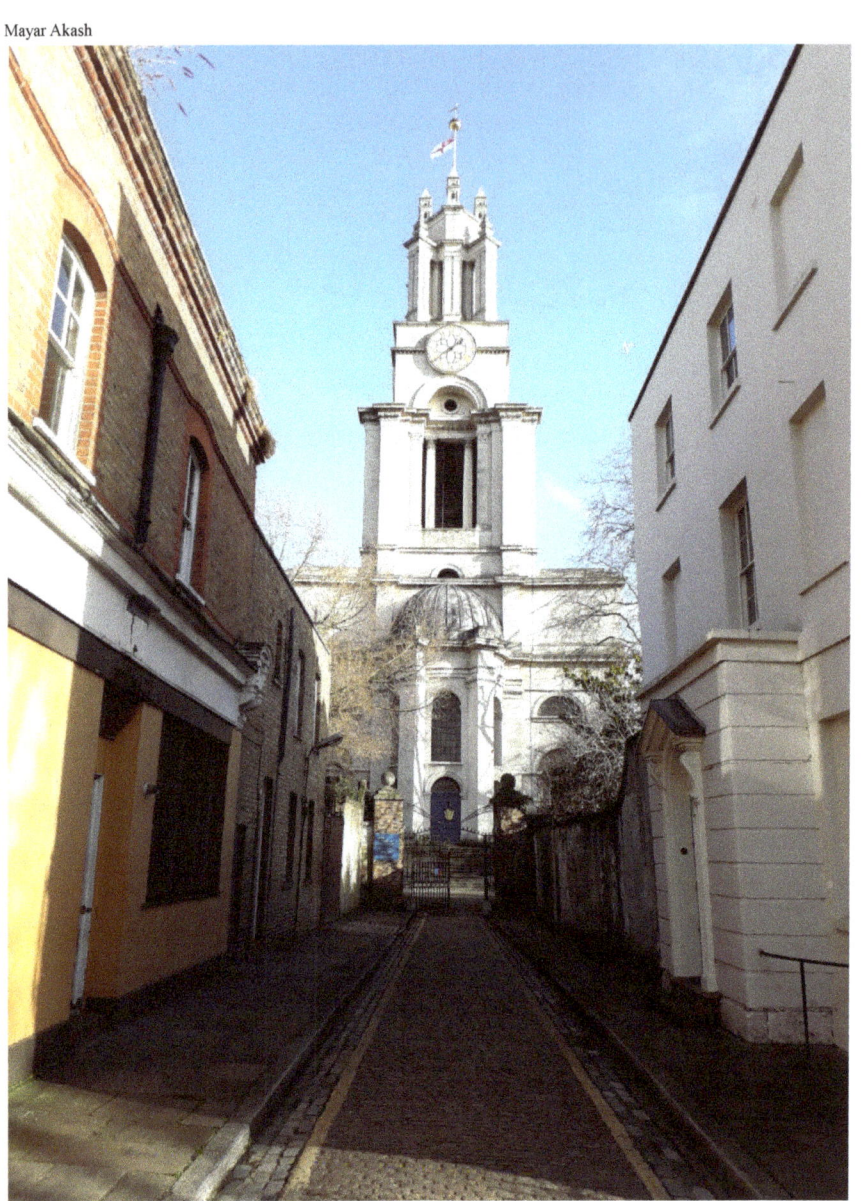

25.1.2018 - 13:36:40

East End Photos, Through Mayar's Eyes : **Tower Hamlets, Random One**

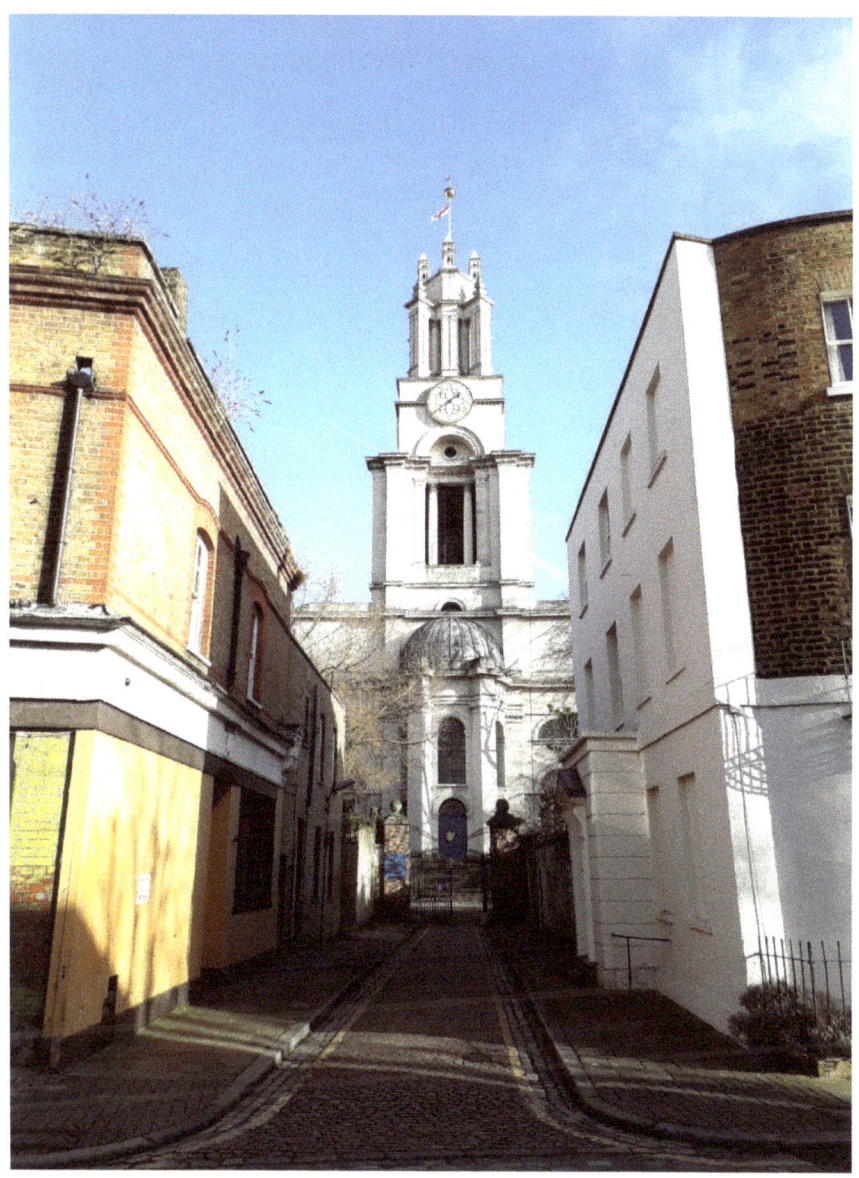

25.1.2018 -13:37:19

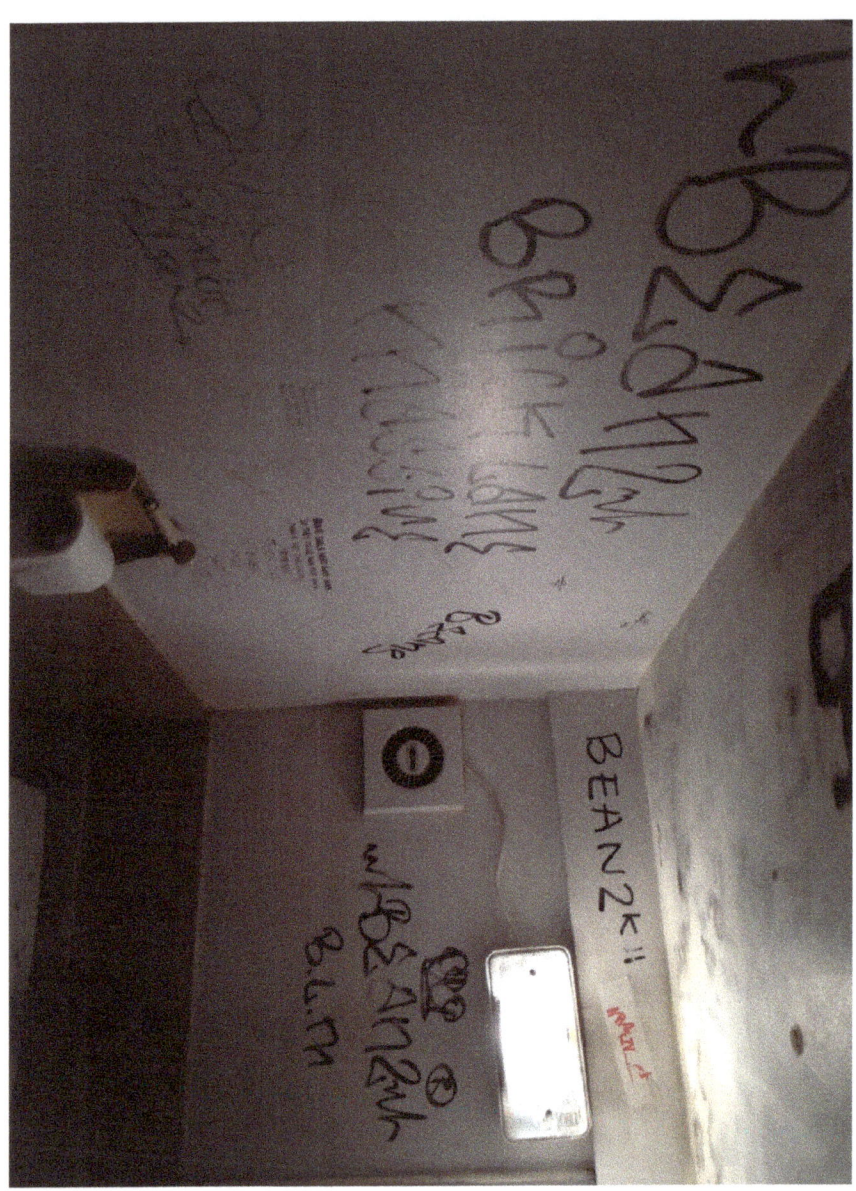

23.3.2014 - 16:08:02

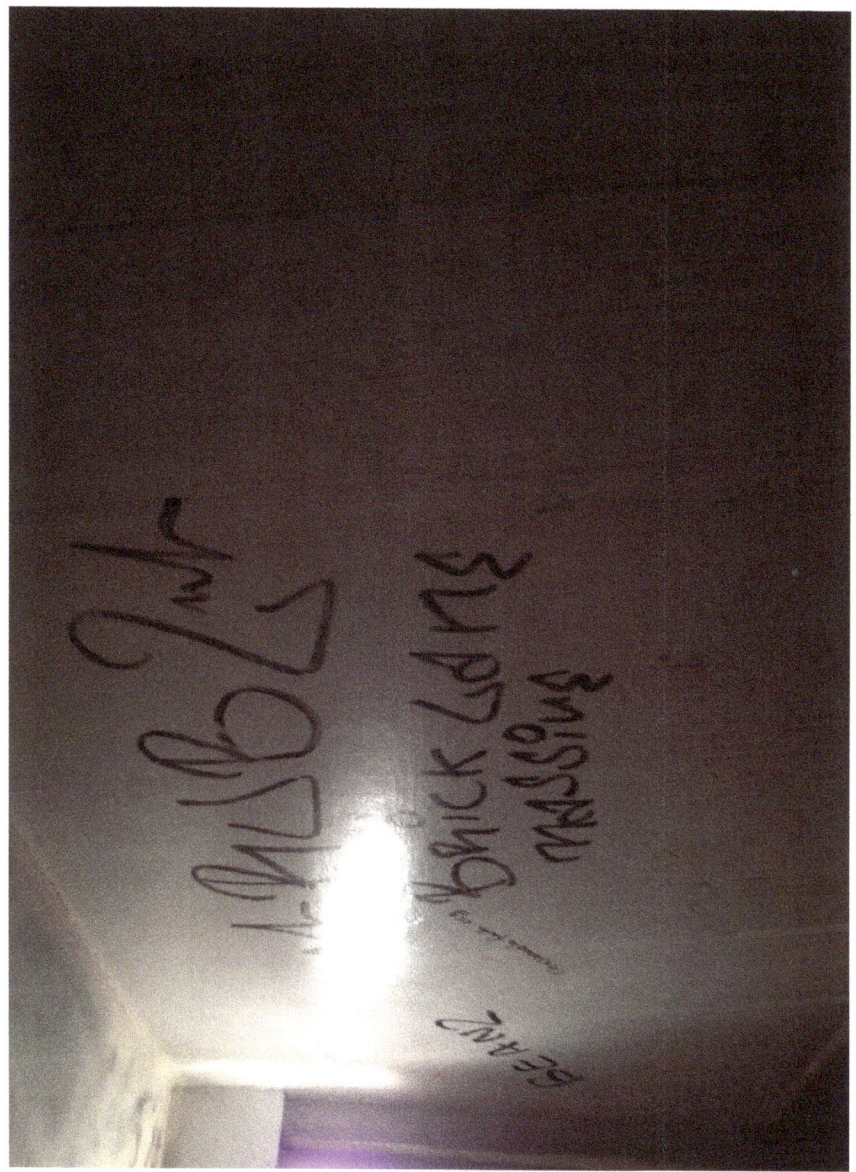

23.3.2014 - 16:08:07

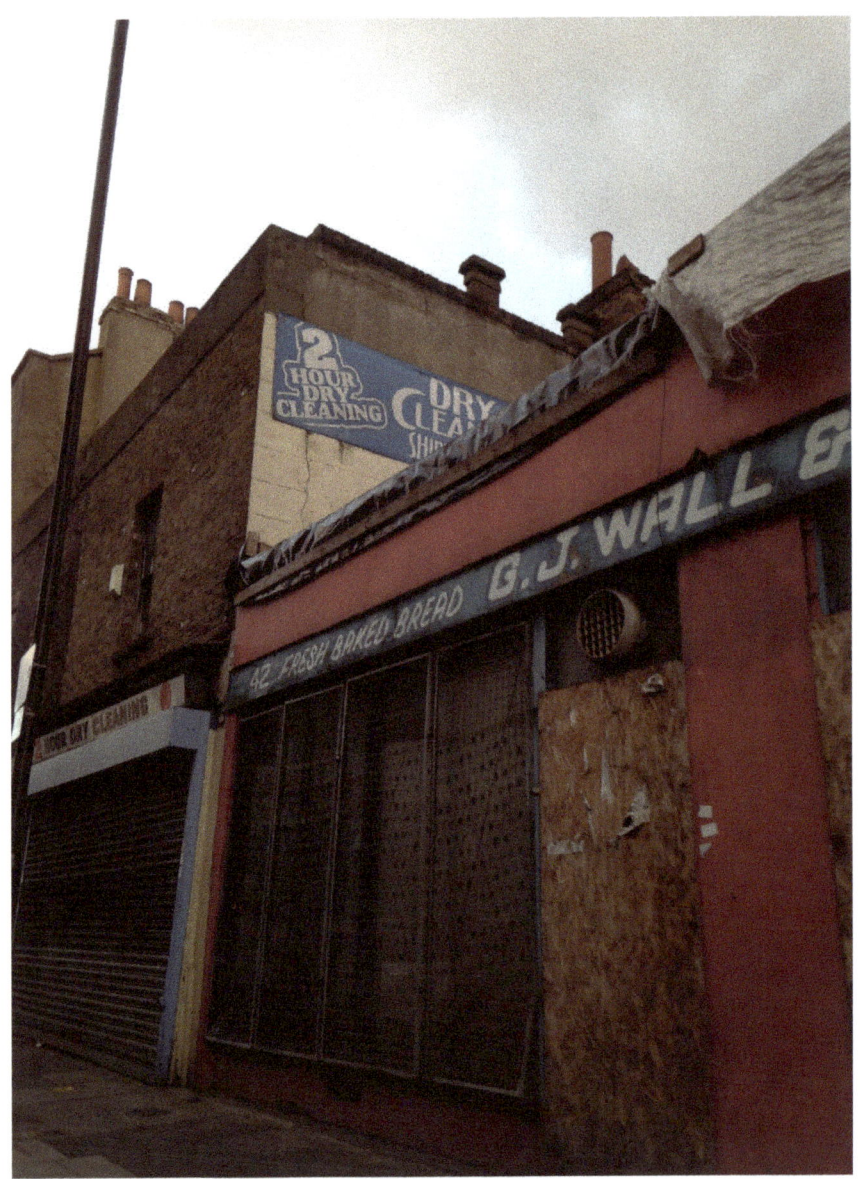

23.3.2014 - 17:03:22

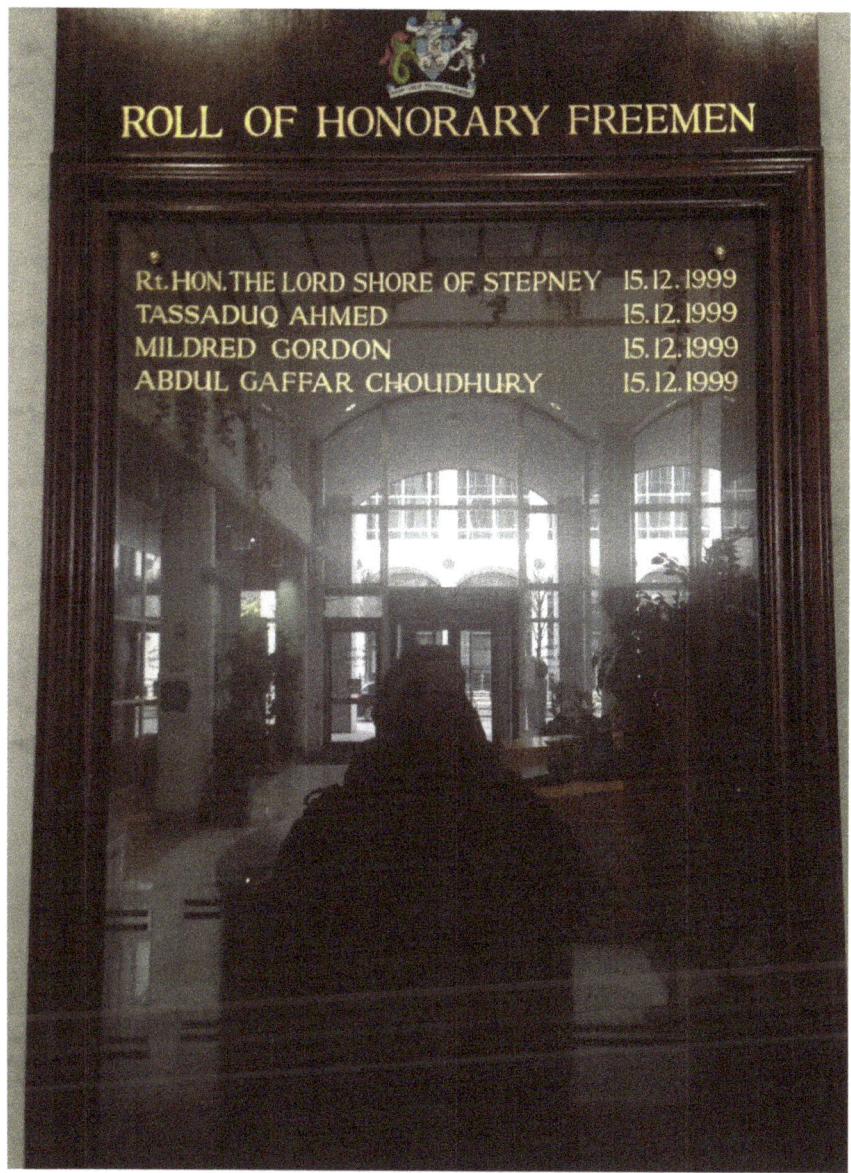

28.3.2014 - 11:33:26, Town Hall Lobby

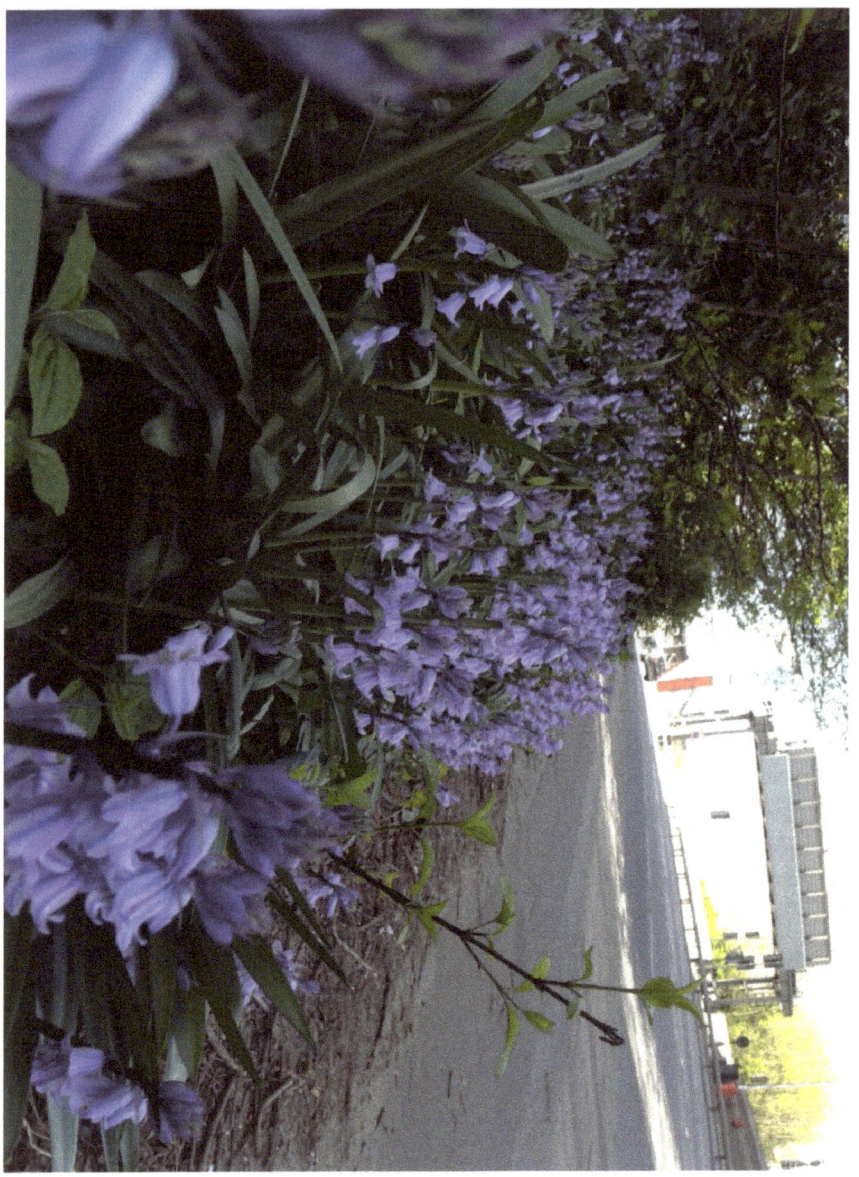

15.4.2014 - 10:41:07,

East End Photos, Through Mayar's Eyes : **Tower Hamlets, Random One**

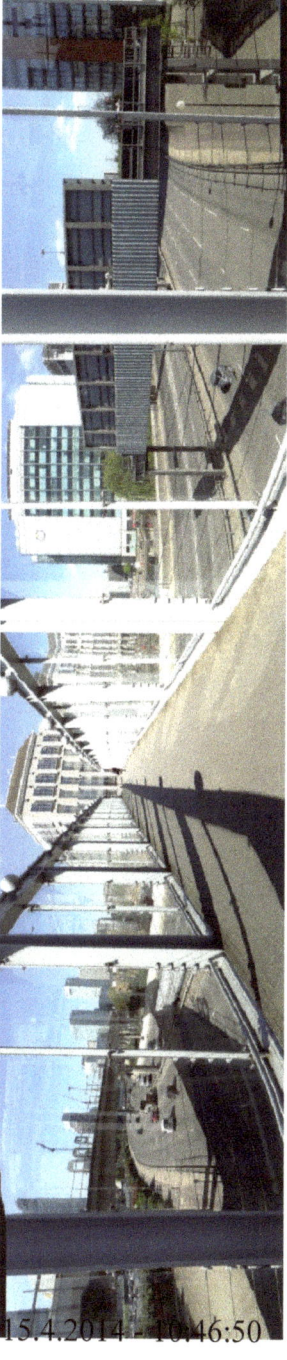

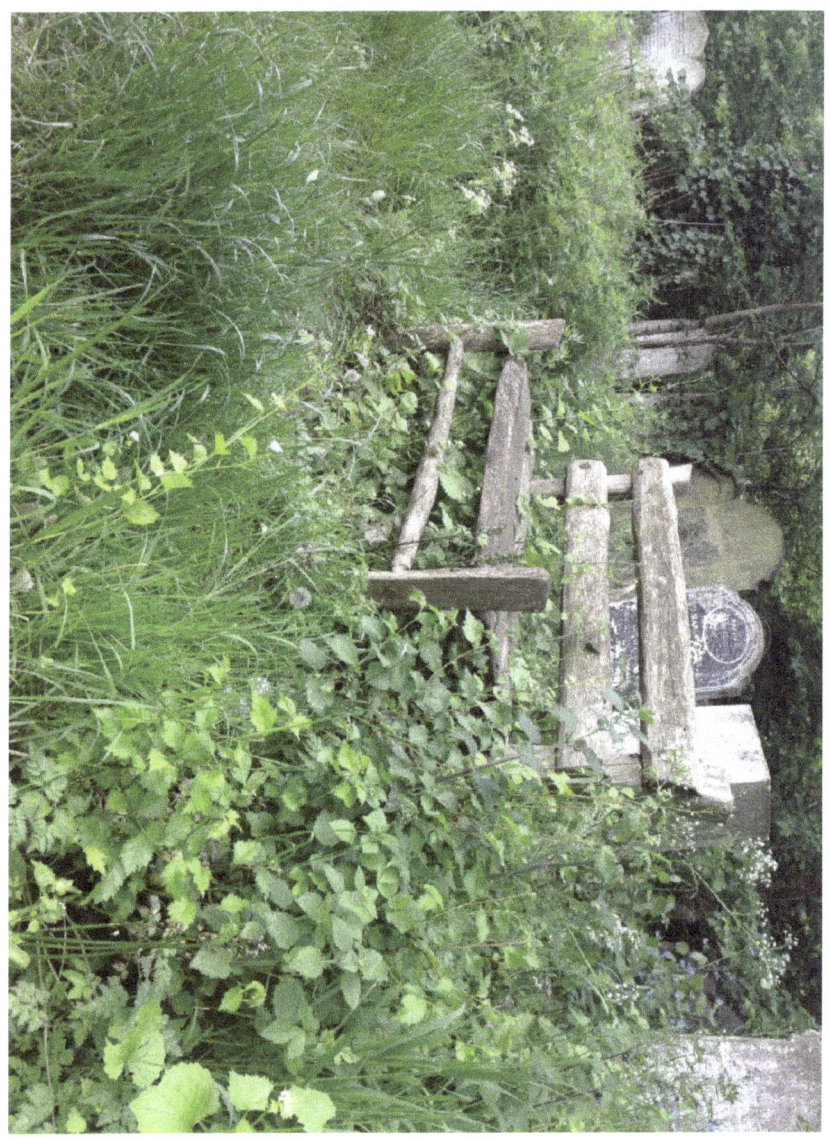

23.5.2016 - 13:27, Tower Hamlets Cemetery Park

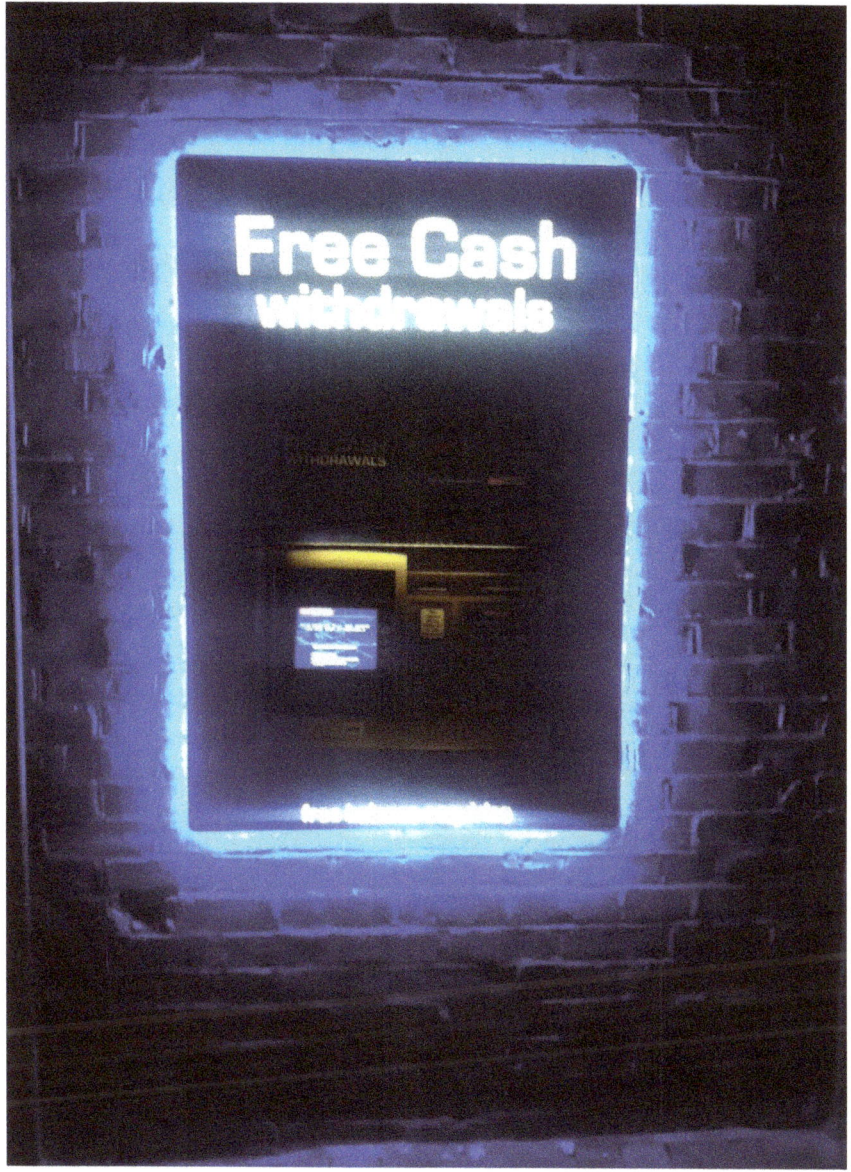

3.12.2012 - 18:00:00, Shadwell, Hole in the wall

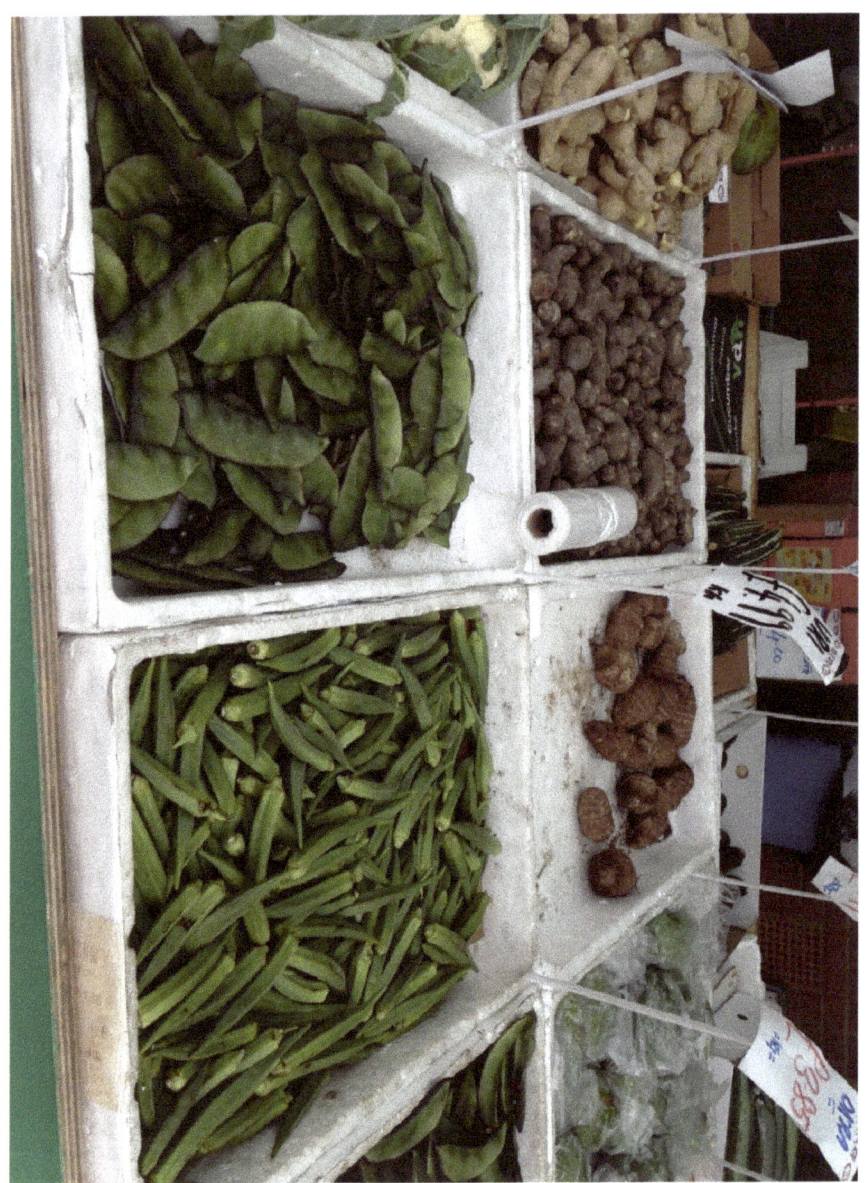

13.7.2014 - 14:57:40, Chapman Street,

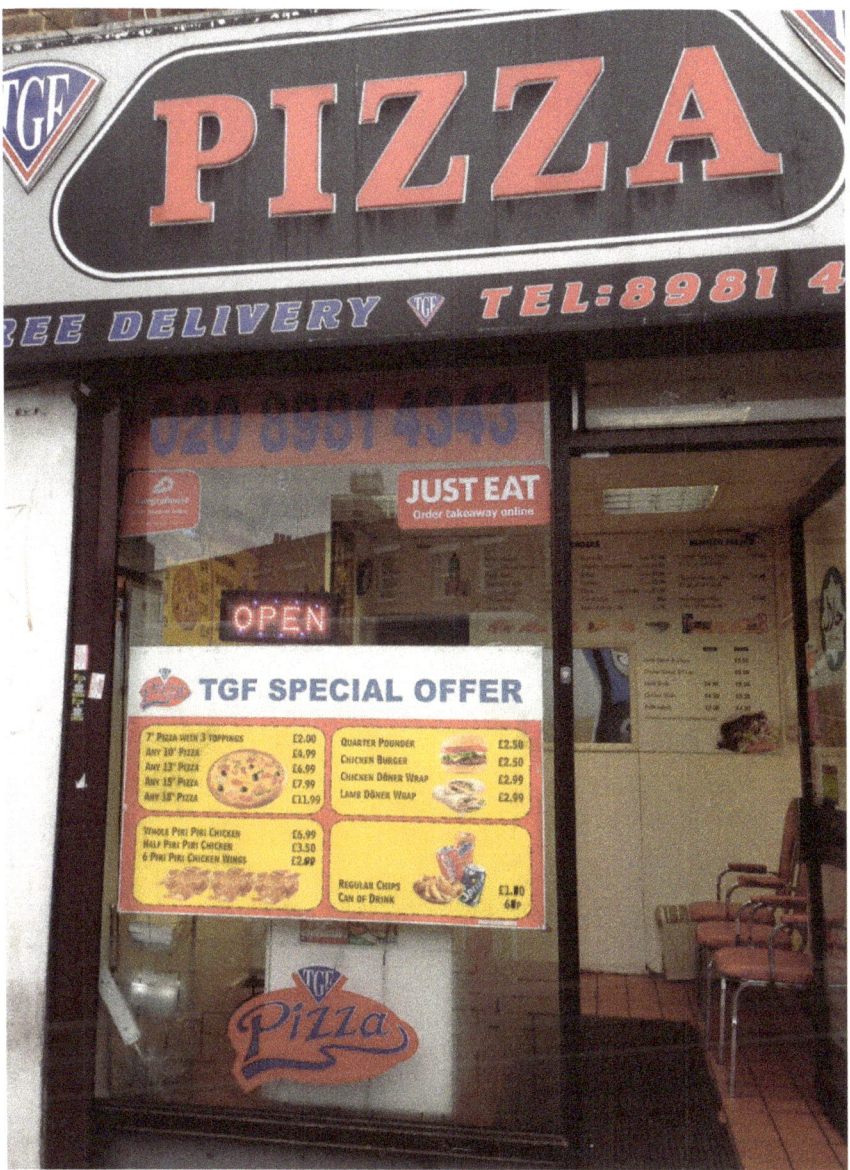

6.9.2016 - 14:10, TGF Pizza, Burdett Road.

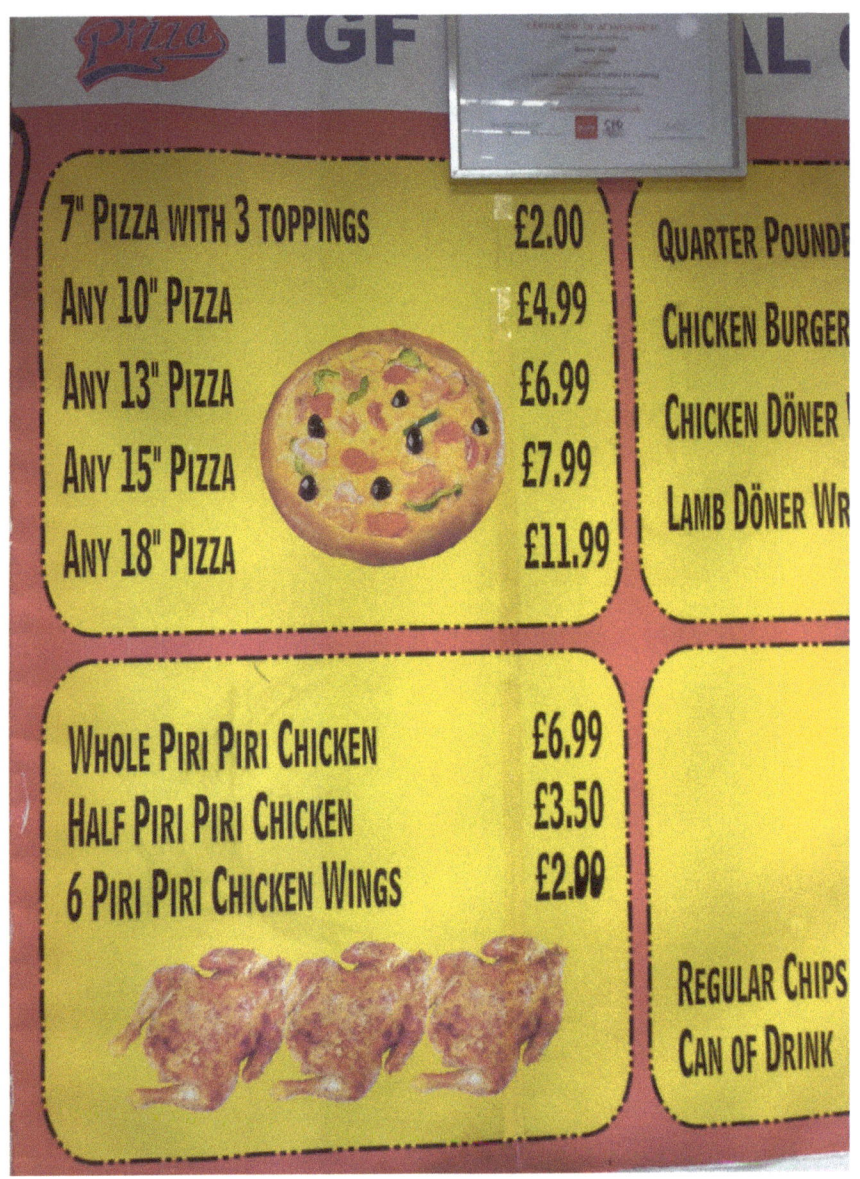

6.9.2016 - 14:10

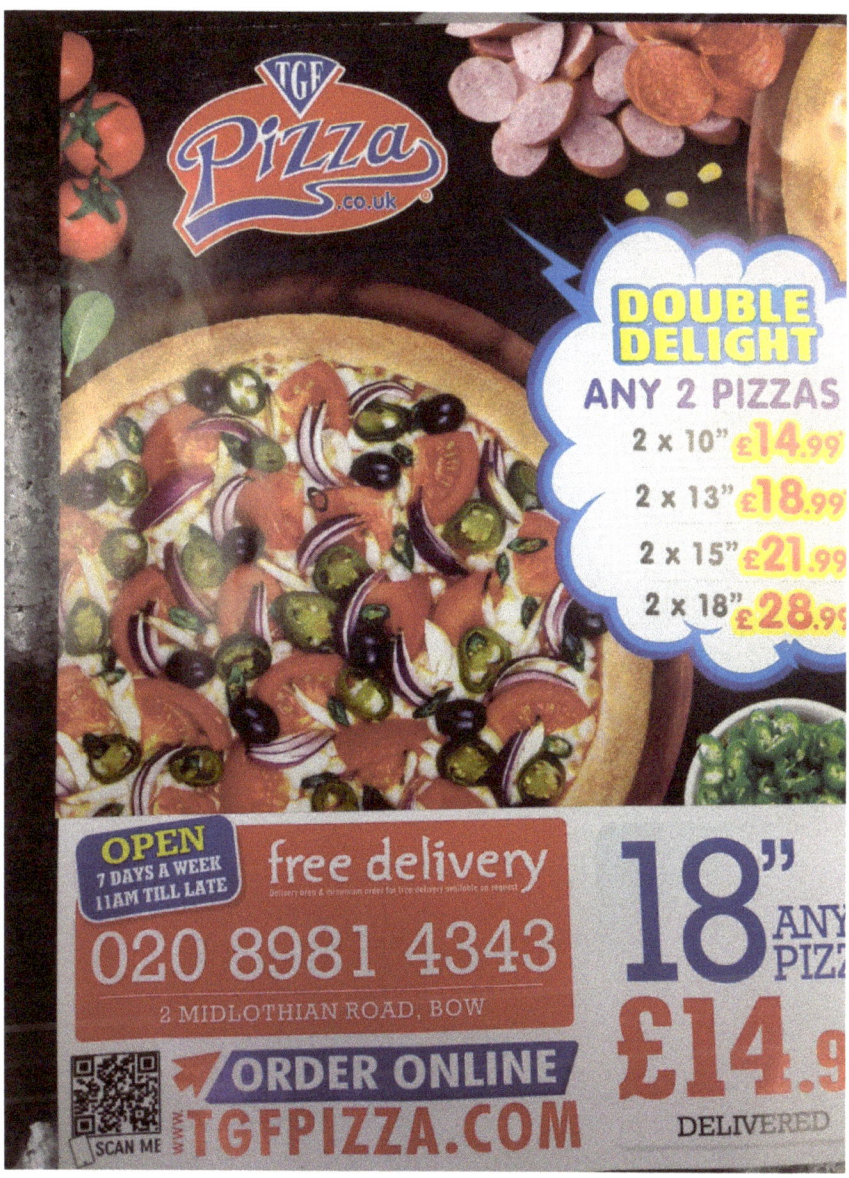

6.9.2016 - 14:10

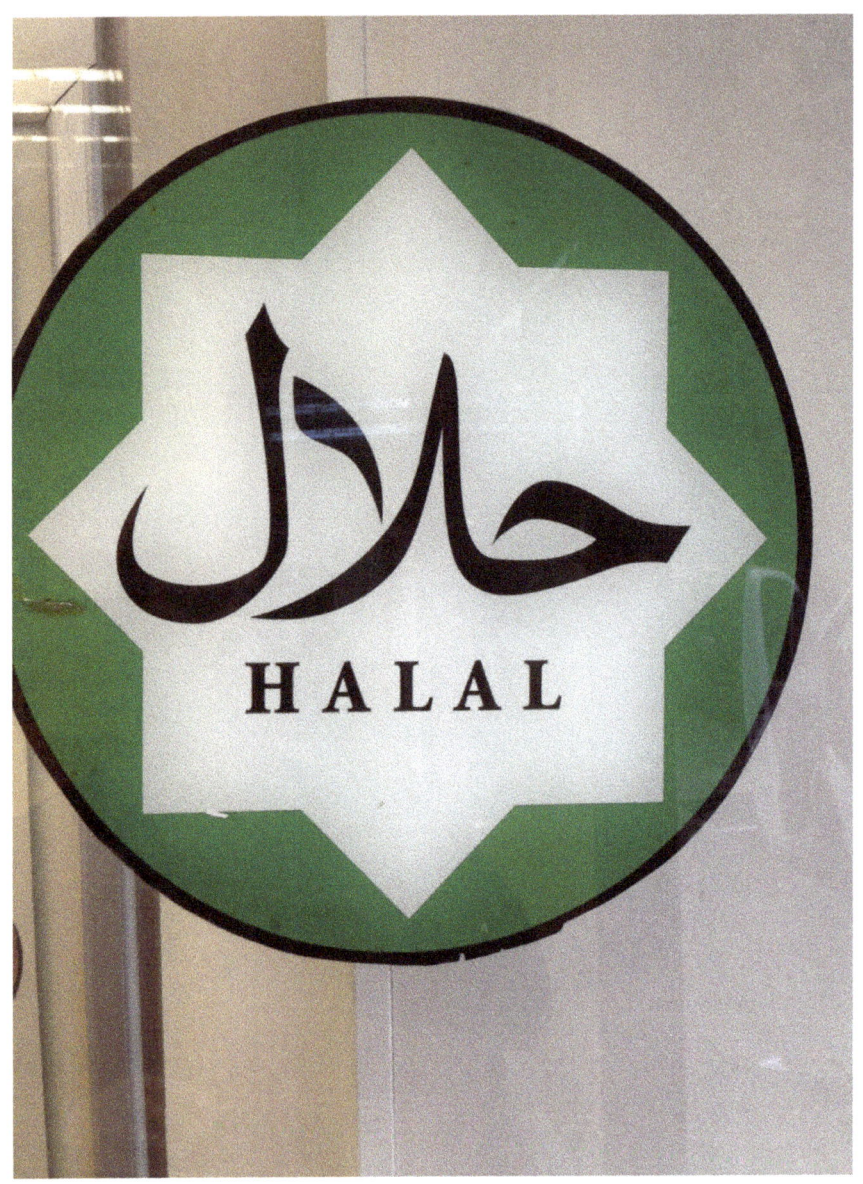

6.9.2016 - 14:10

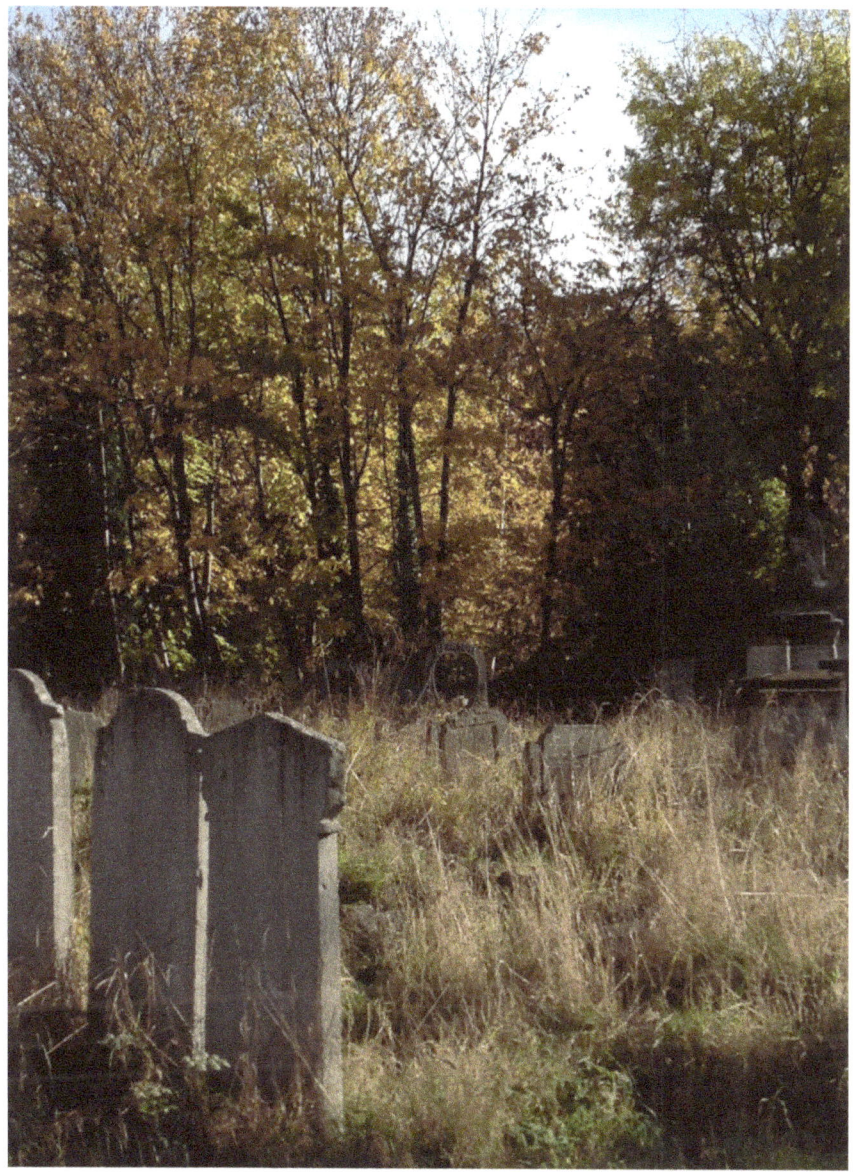

16.11.2016 - 11:10:07, Mile End Cemetery

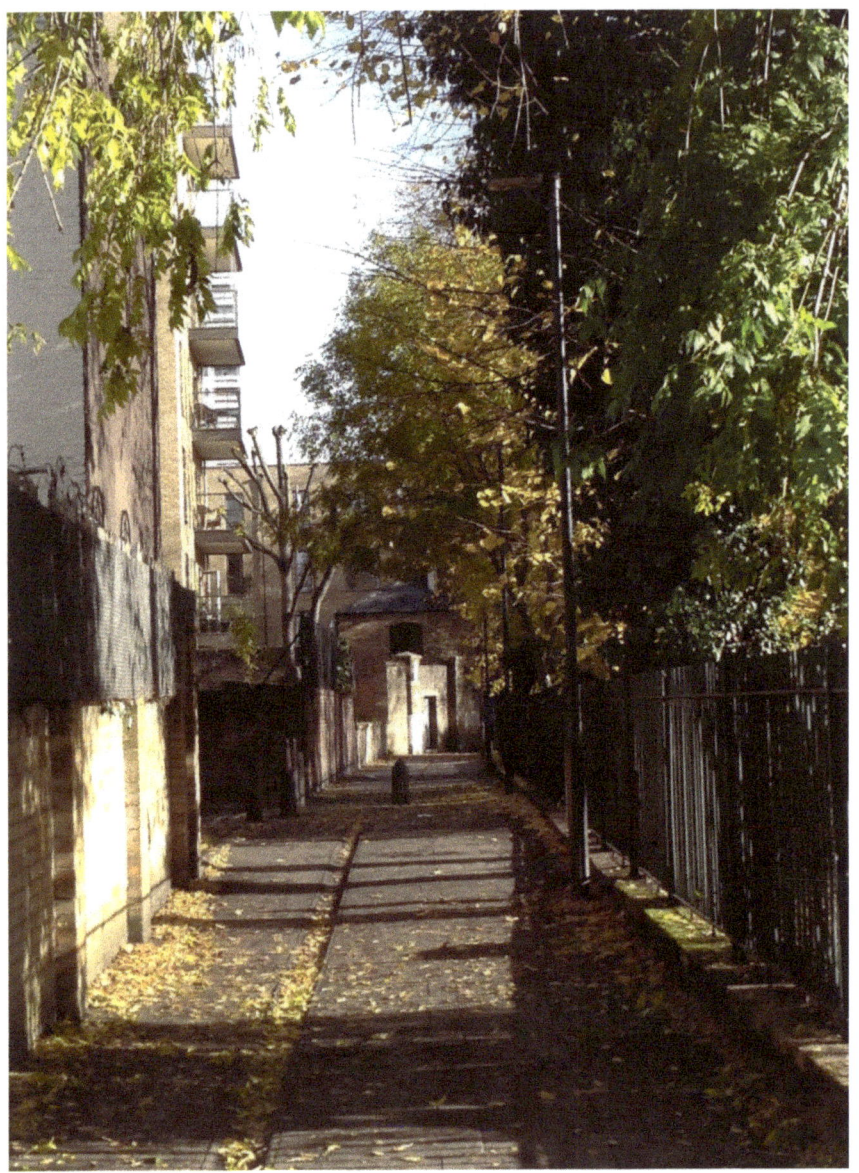

16.11.2016 - 11:10:20, Hamlets Way

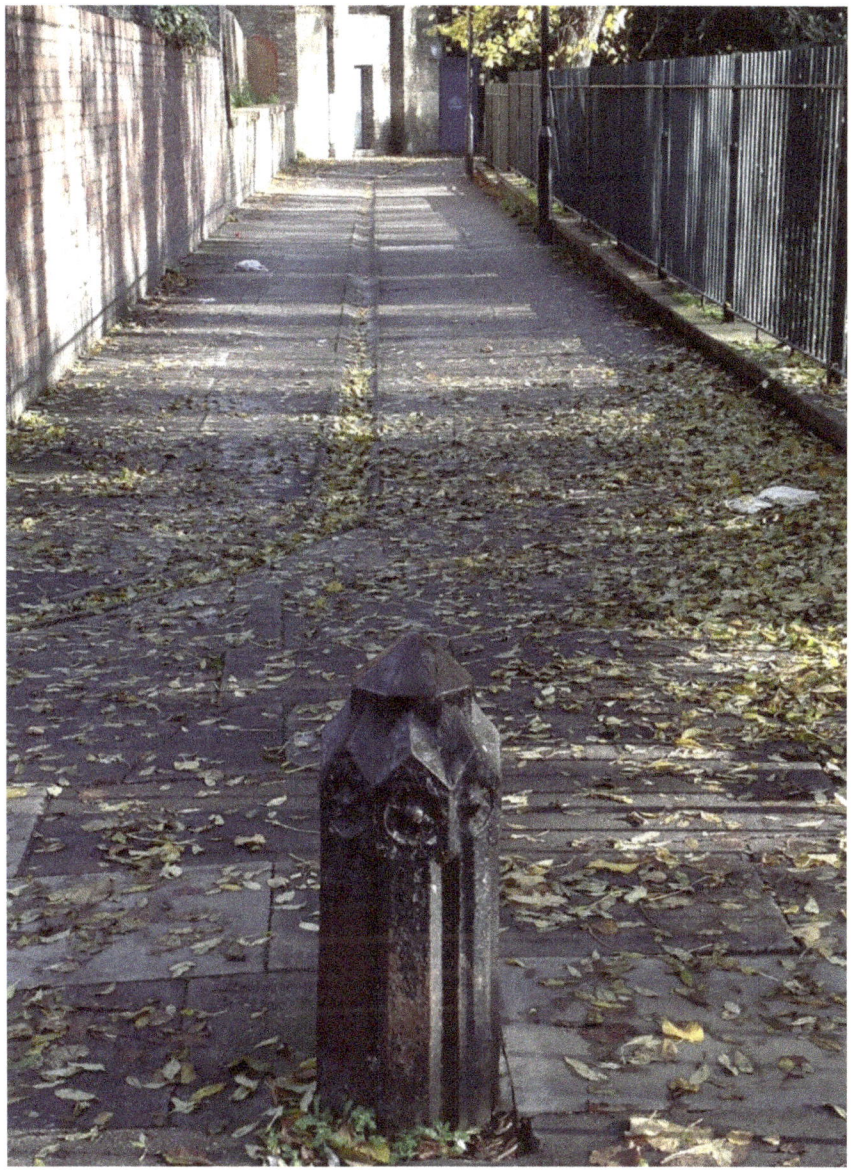

16.11.2016 - 11:10

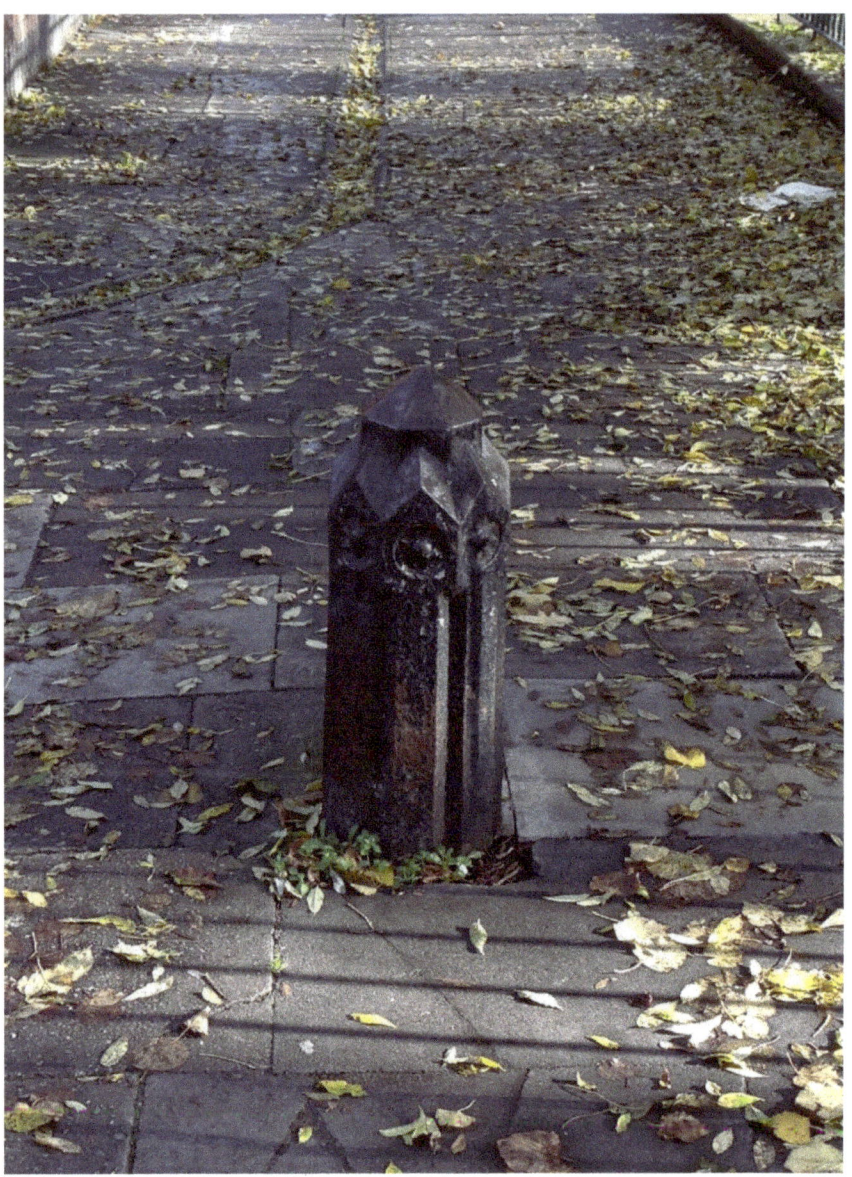

16.11.2016 - 11:10

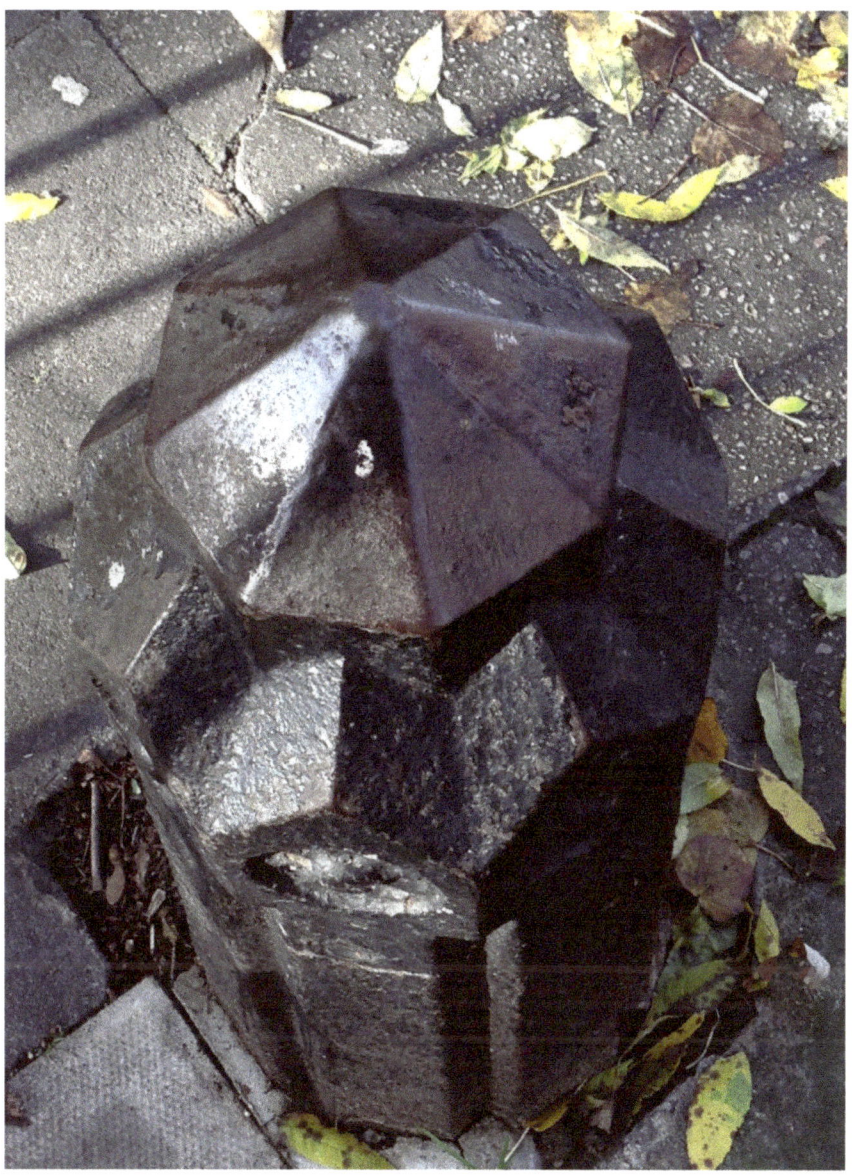

16.11.2016 - 11:11:13

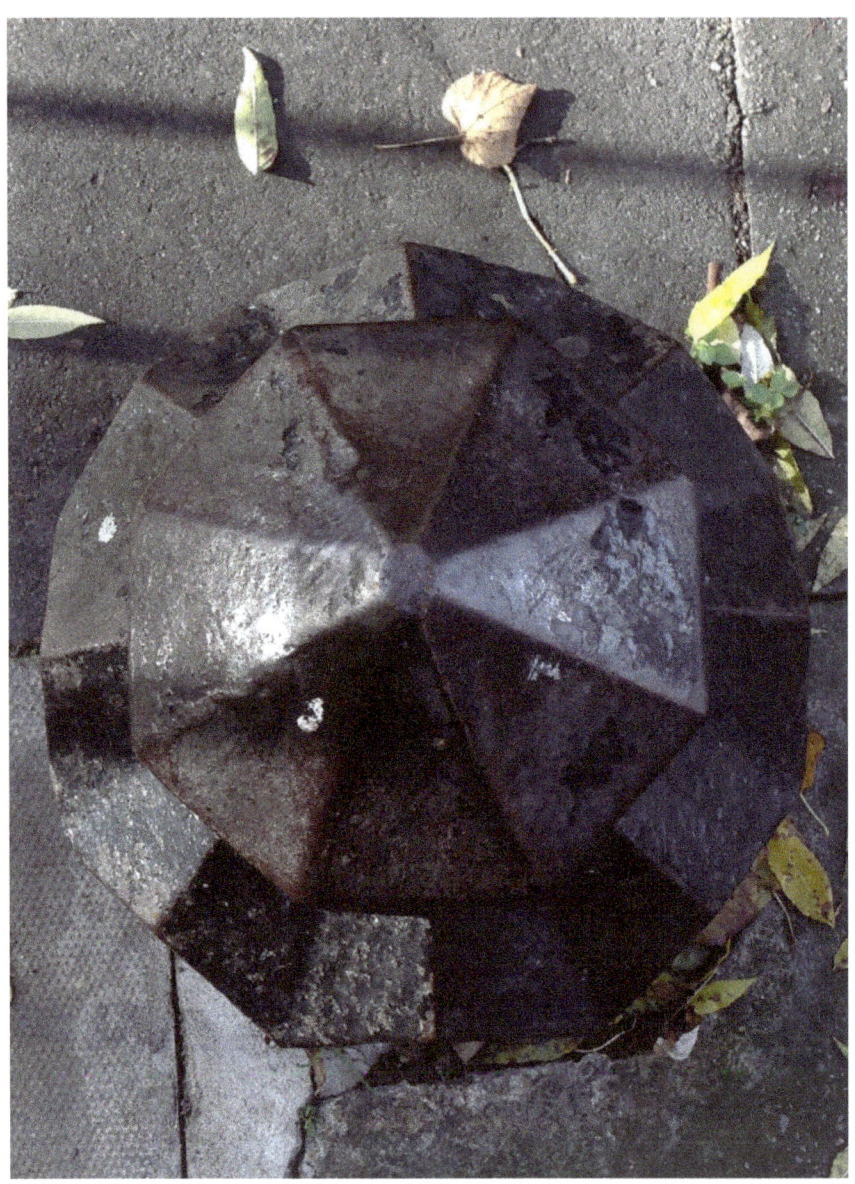

16.11.2016 - 11:11:22

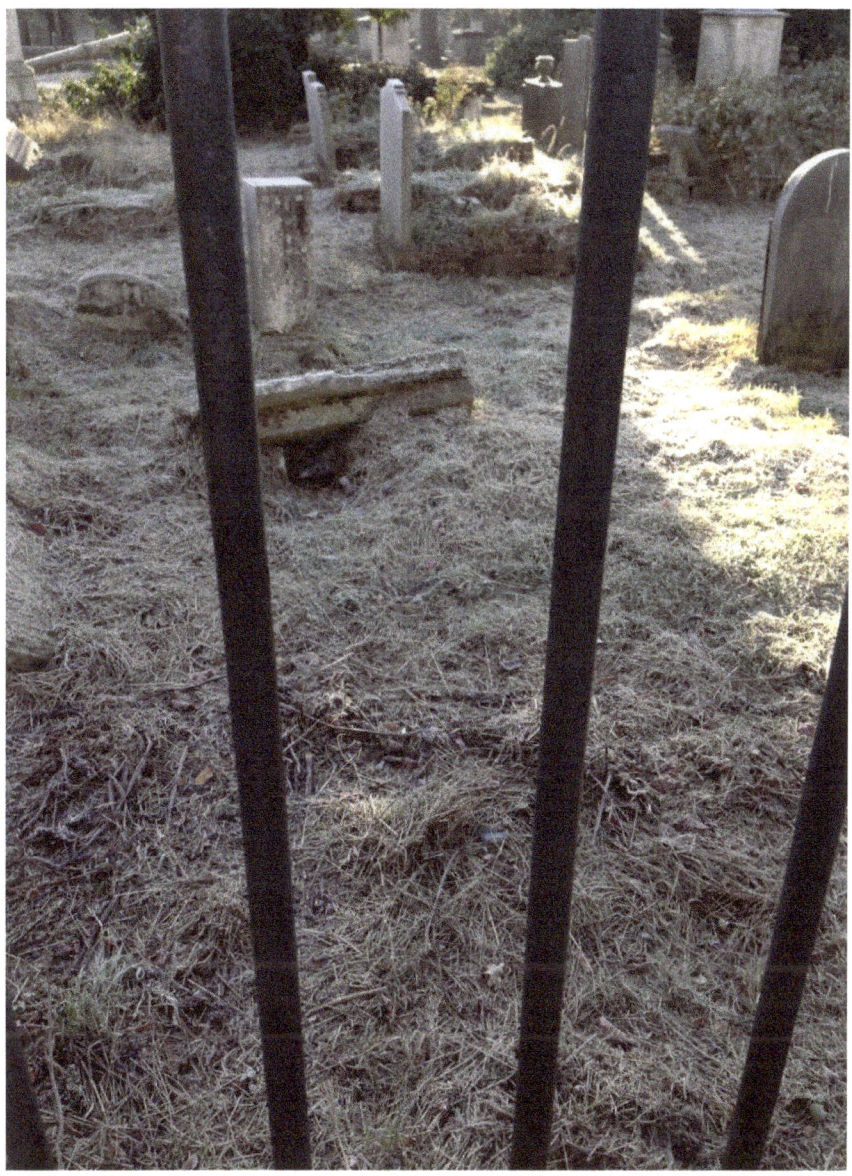

30.11.2016 - 10:43:18

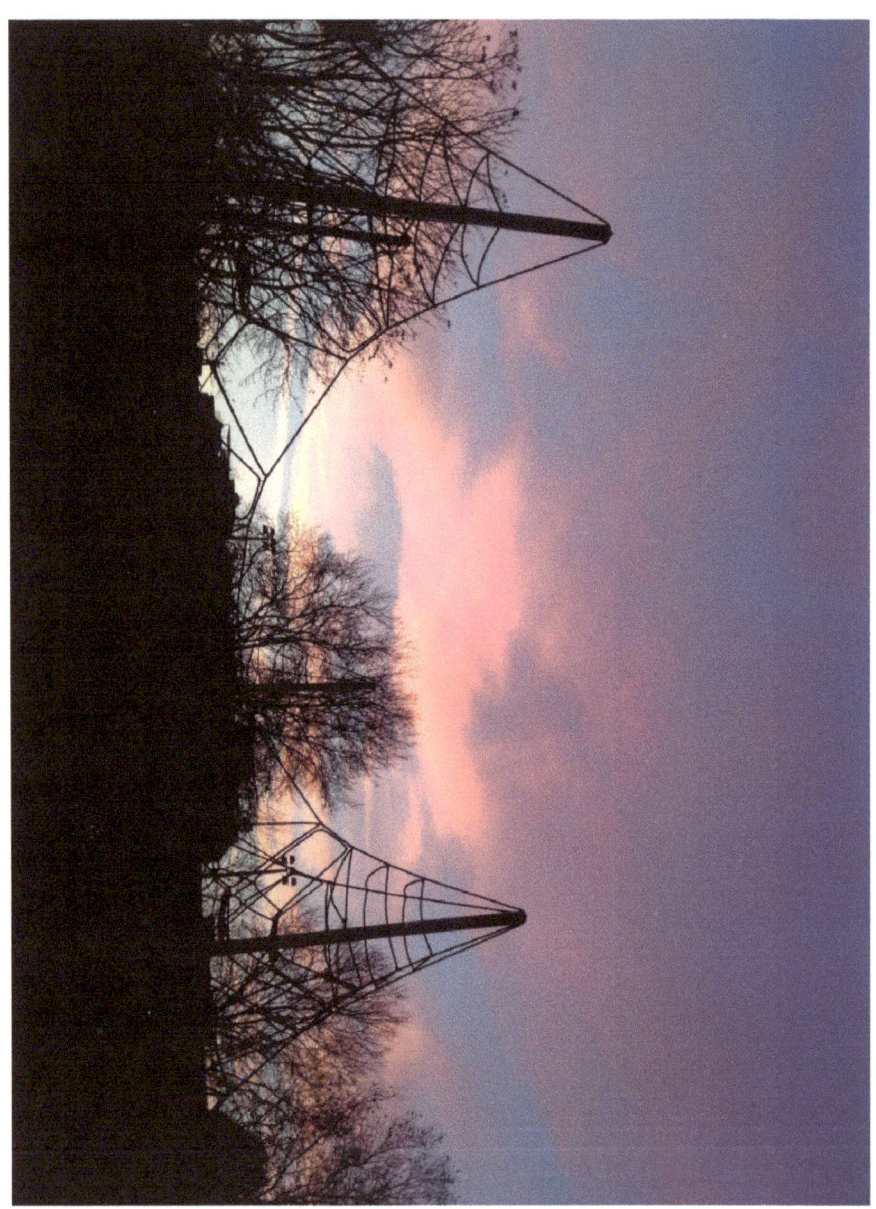

30.11.2016 - 16:15:53, Mile End park, Burdett road.

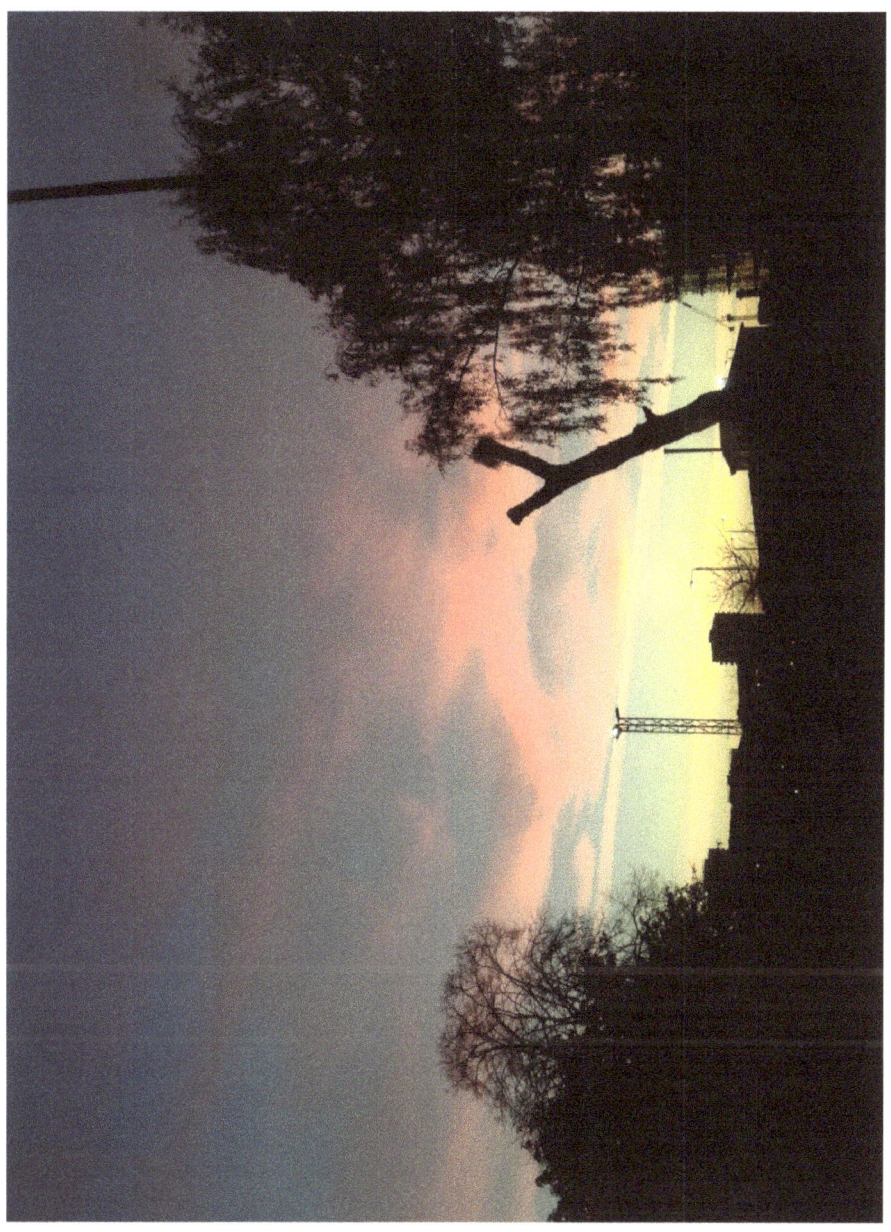

30.11.2016 - 16:20:00

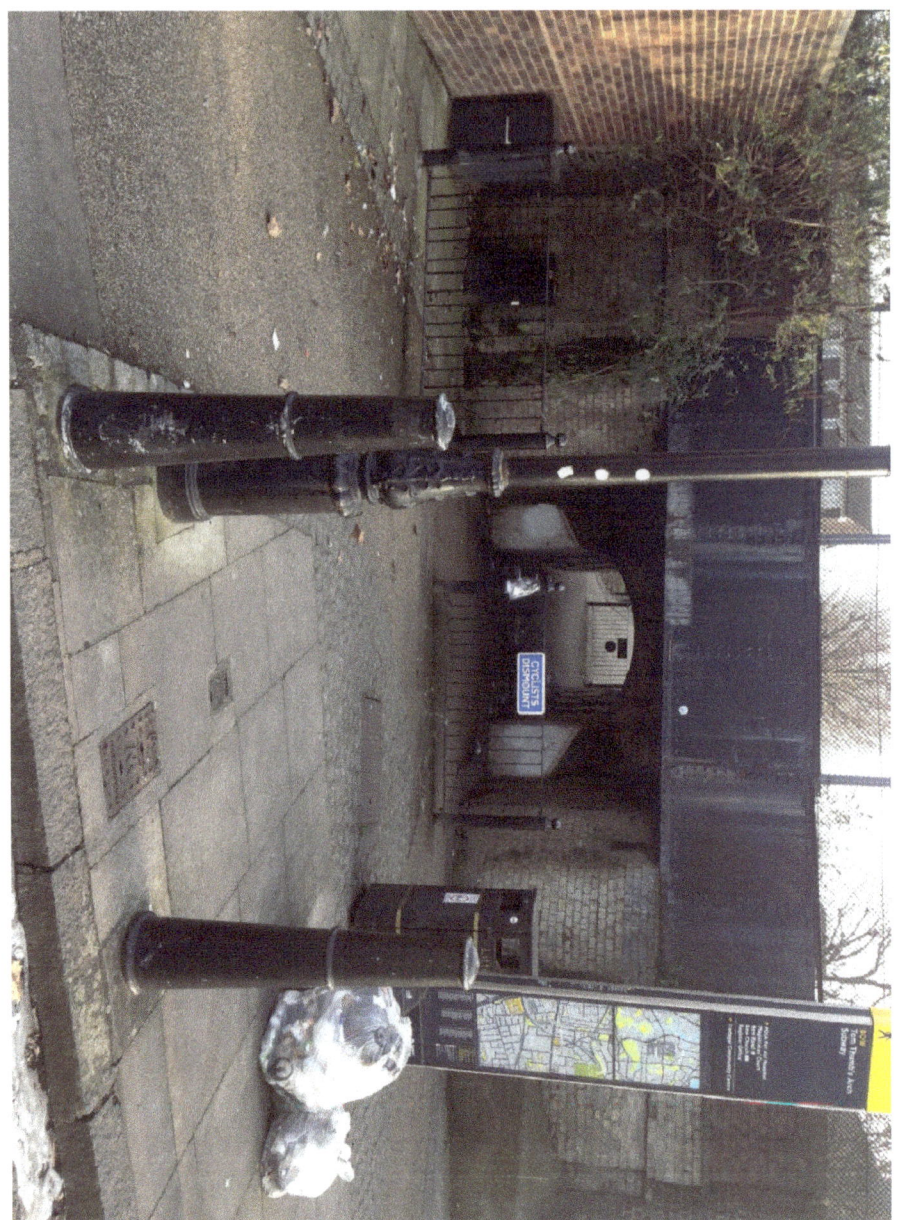

13.2.2017 - 15:45, Tom Thumb's Arch subway, Bow

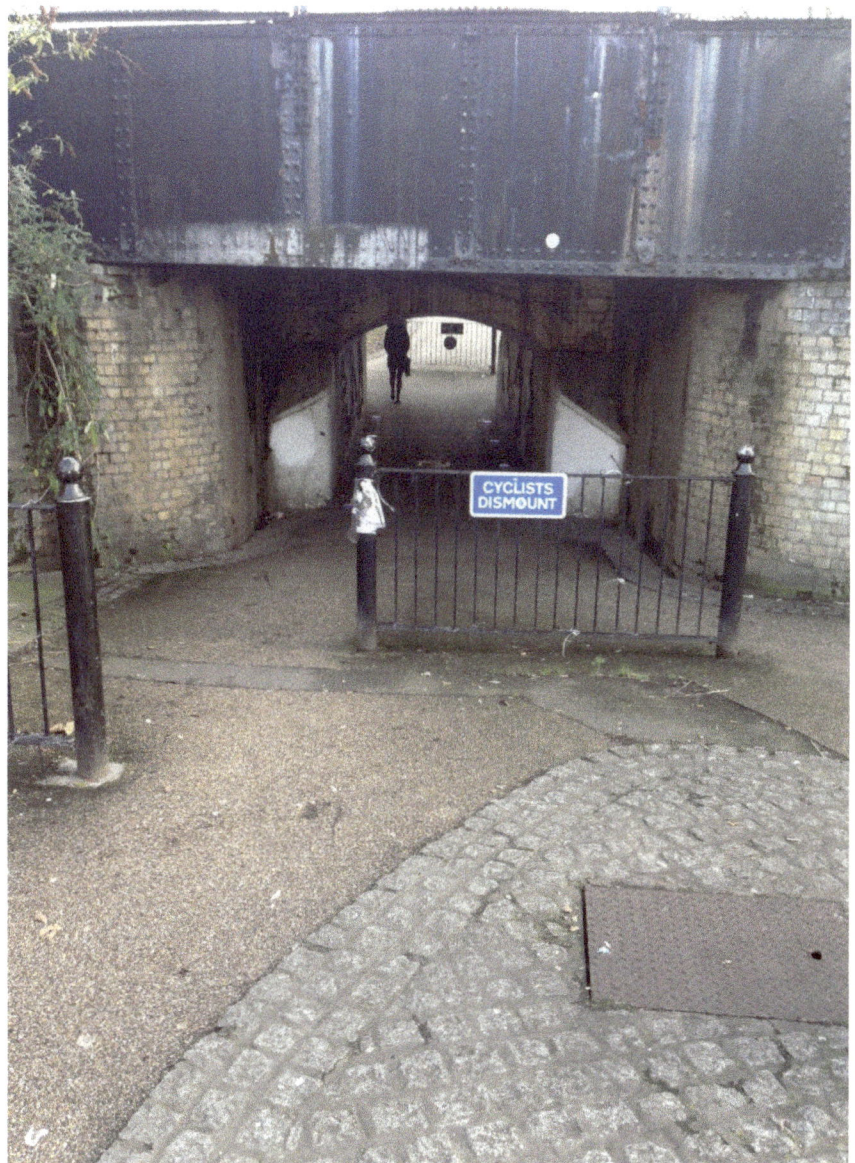

13.2.2017 - 15:45, Tom Thumb's Arch subway, Bow

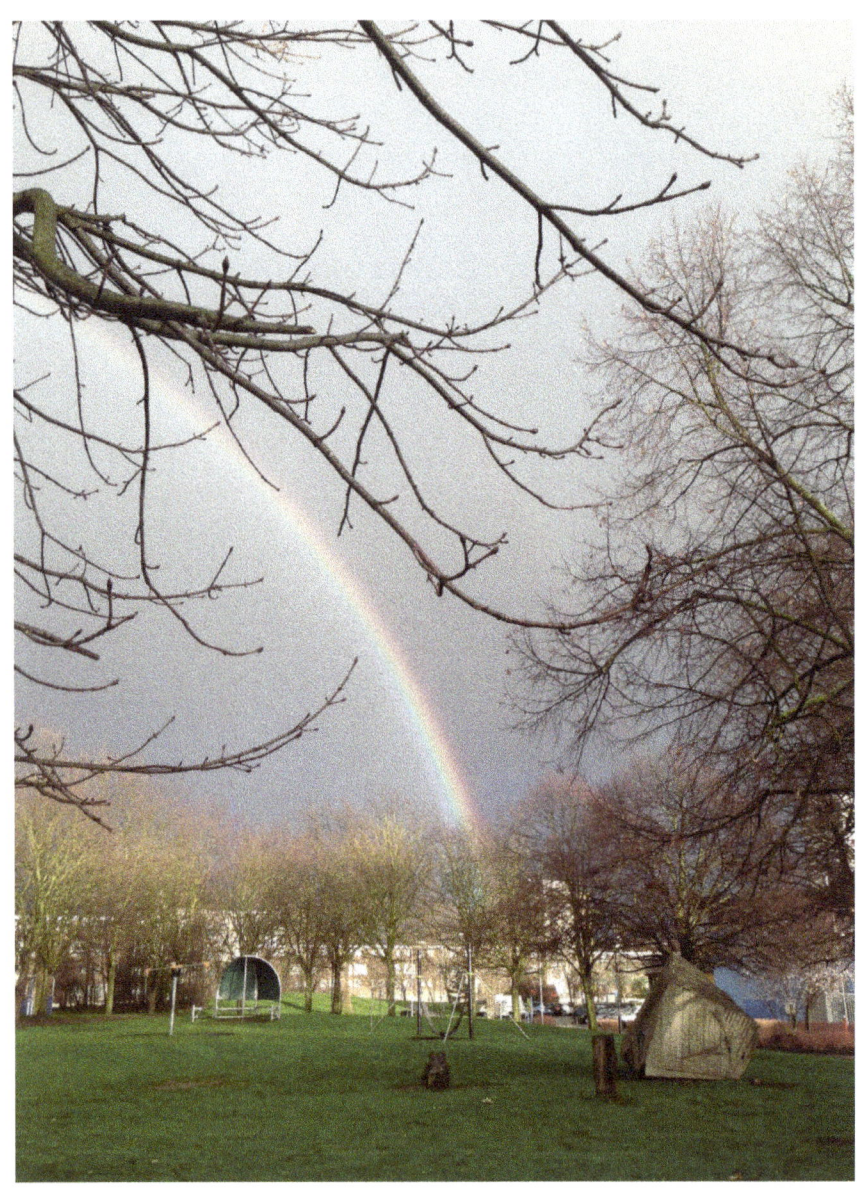

27.2.2017 - 17:00, Mile End Park, Burdette road

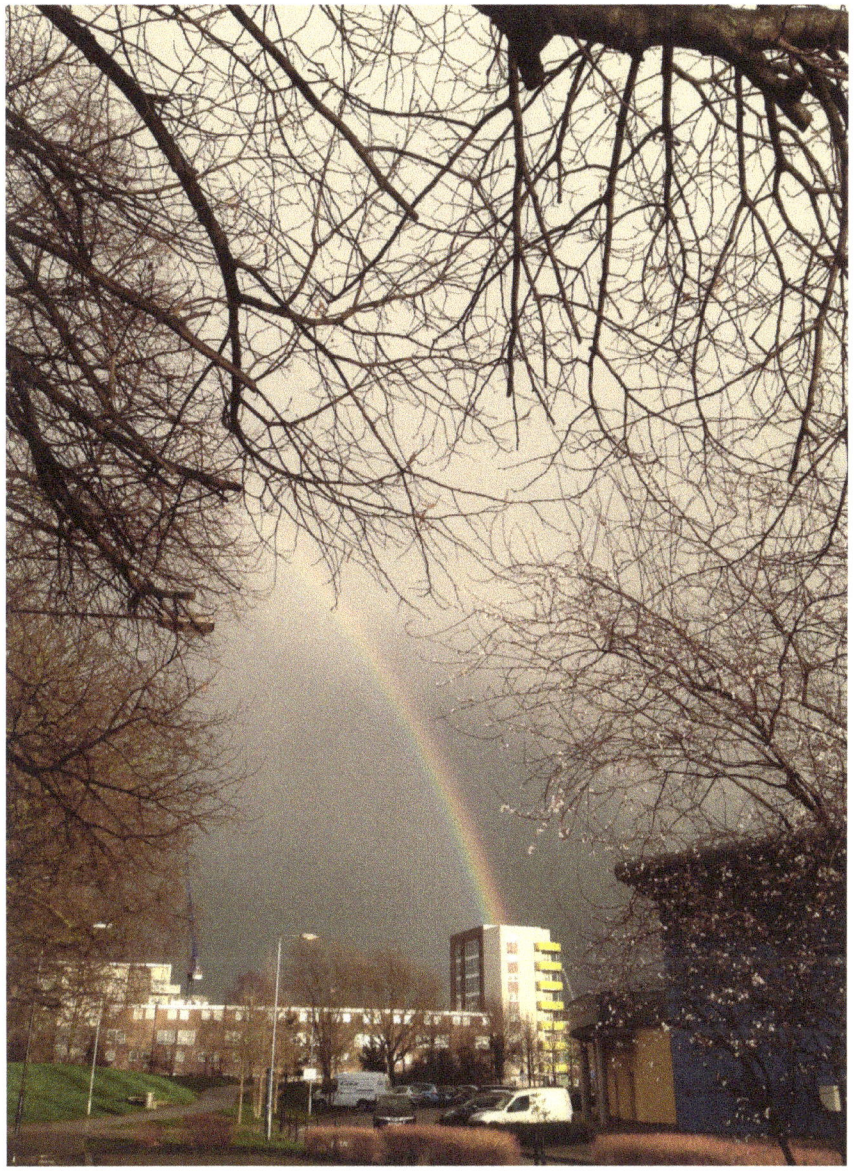

27.2.2017 - 17:02

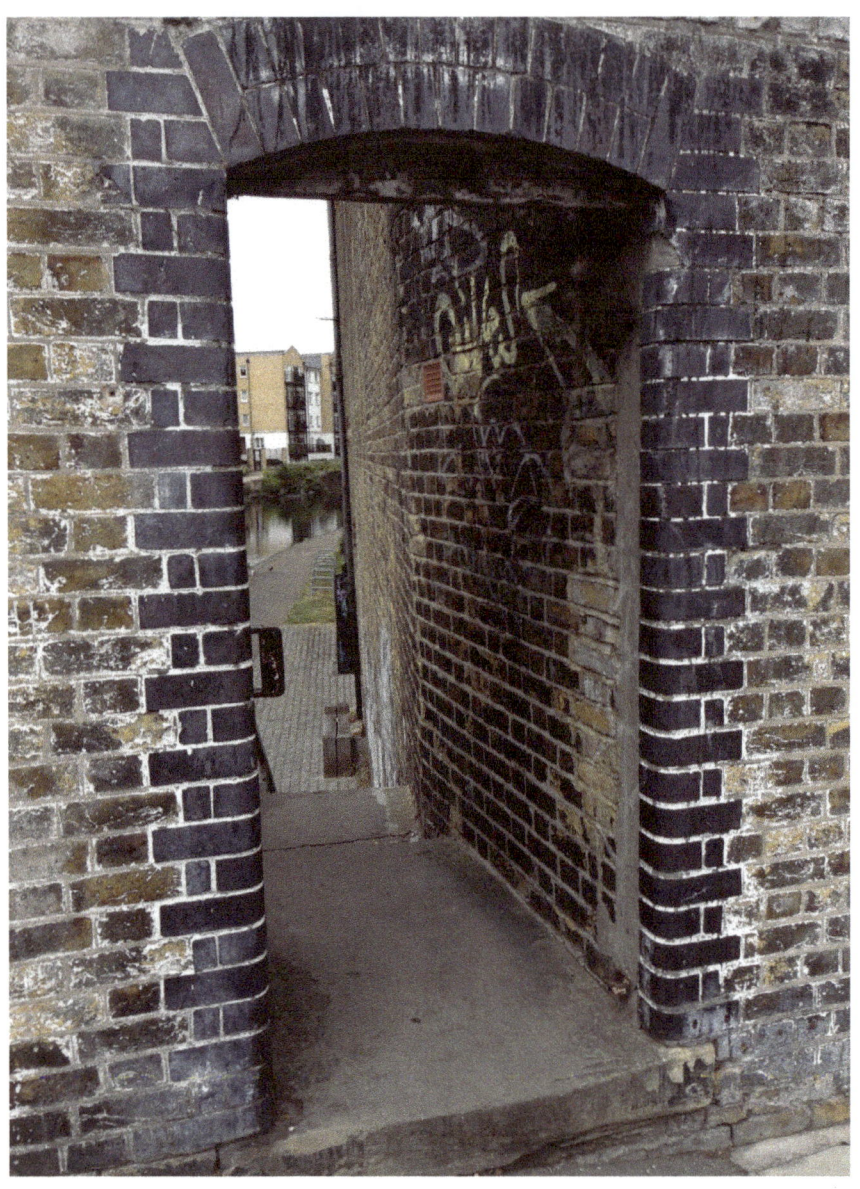

25.6.2015 - 12:56

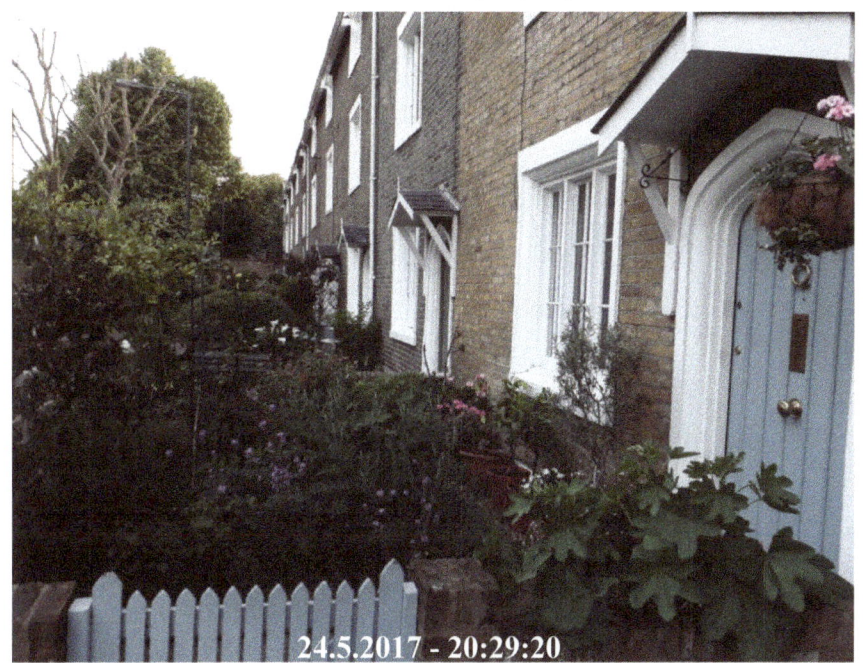

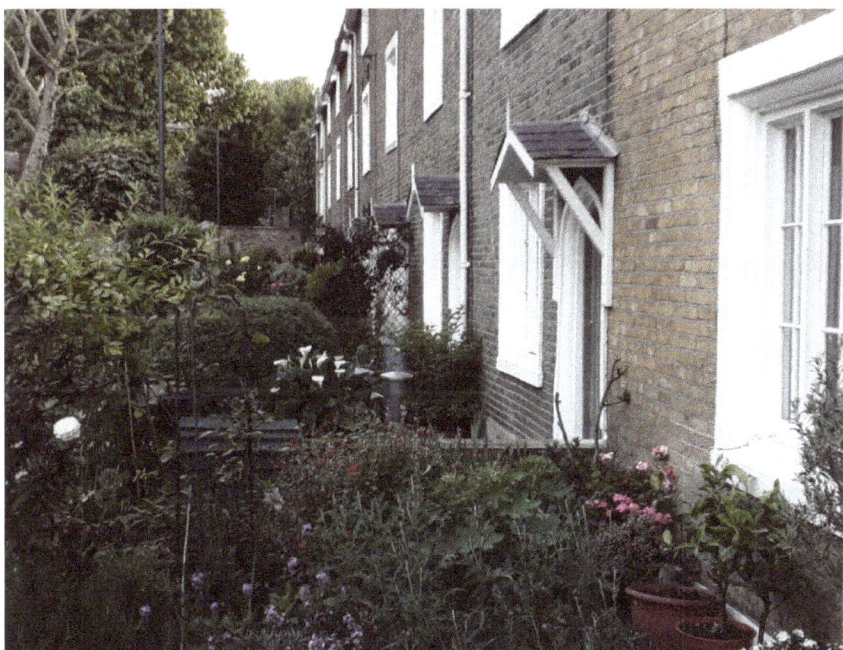

24.5.2017 - 20:29:05, Maria Terrace,

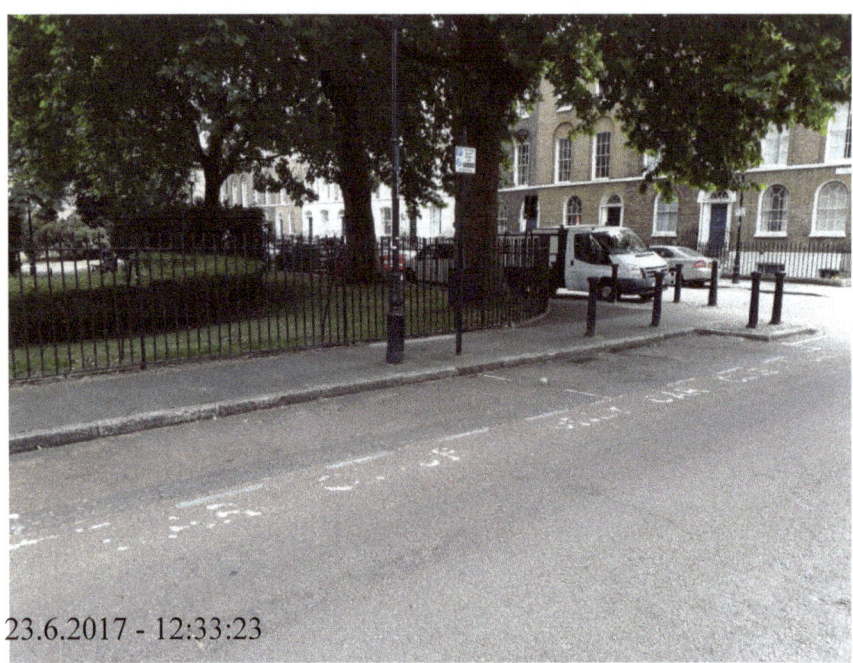

23.6.2017 - 12:33:23

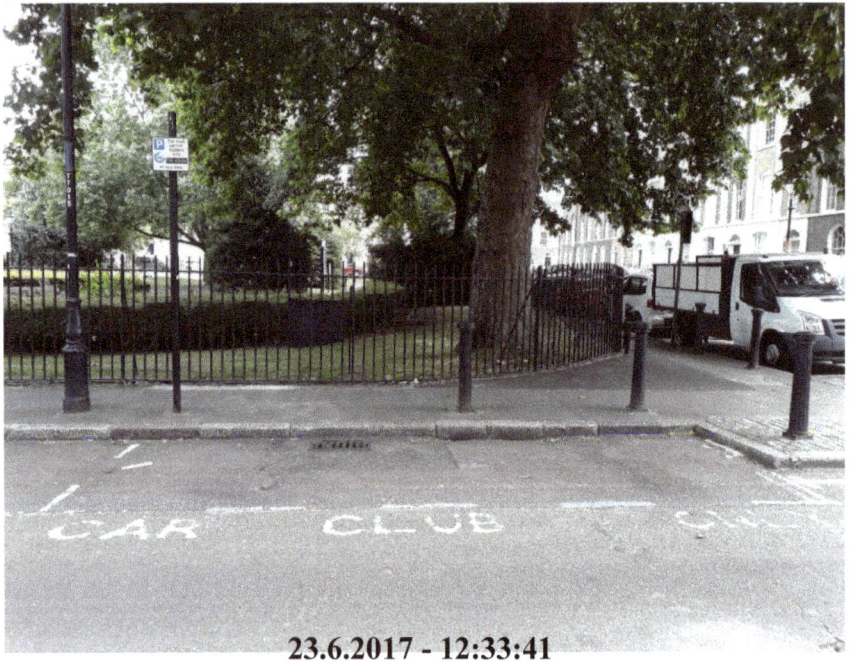

23.6.2017 - 12:33:41

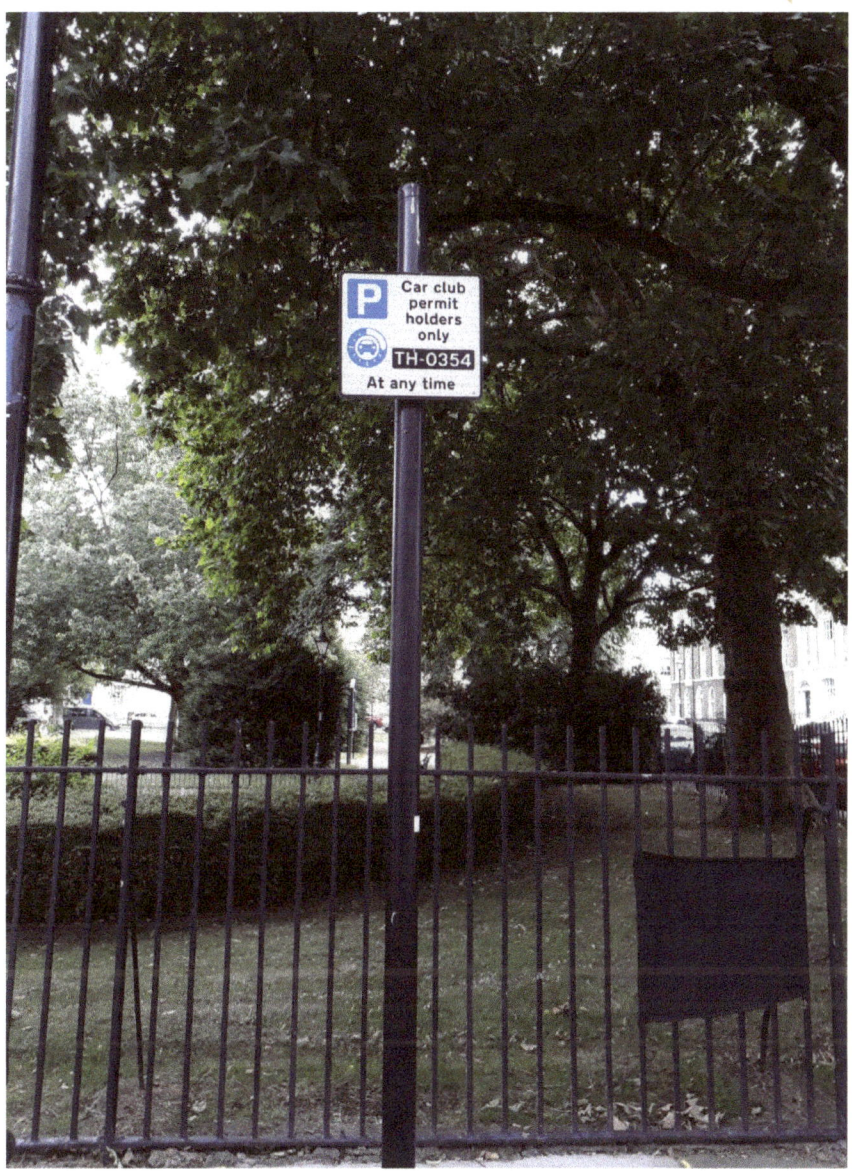

23.6.2017 - 12:34:01

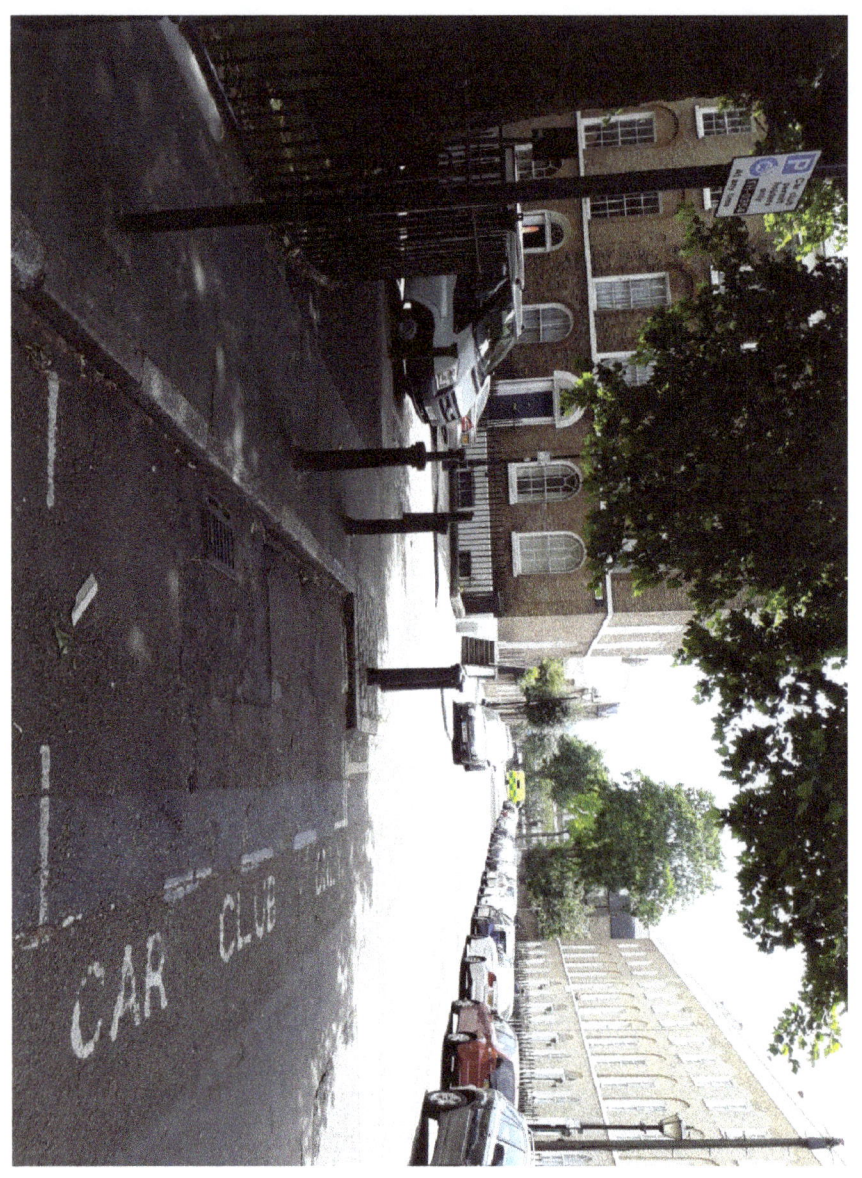

23.6.2017 - 12:34:34, Tredegar Square

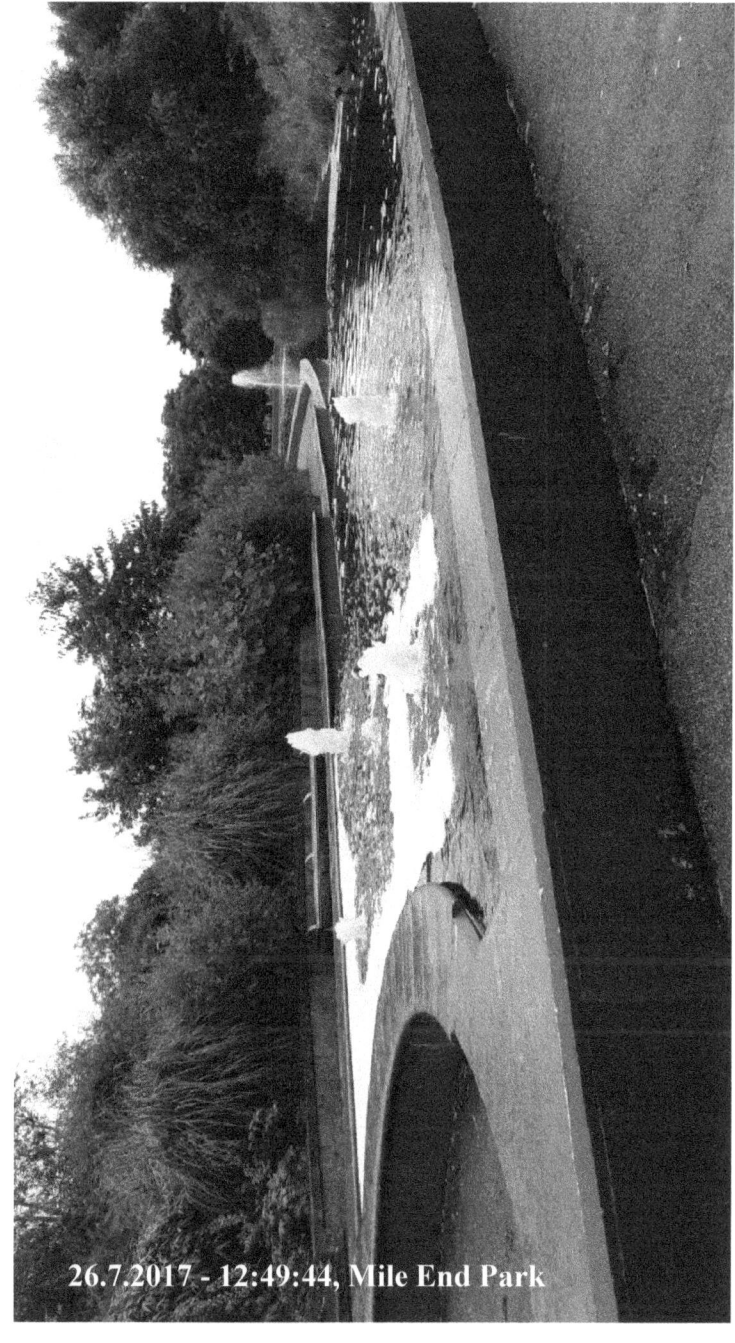

26.7.2017 - 12:49:44, Mile End Park

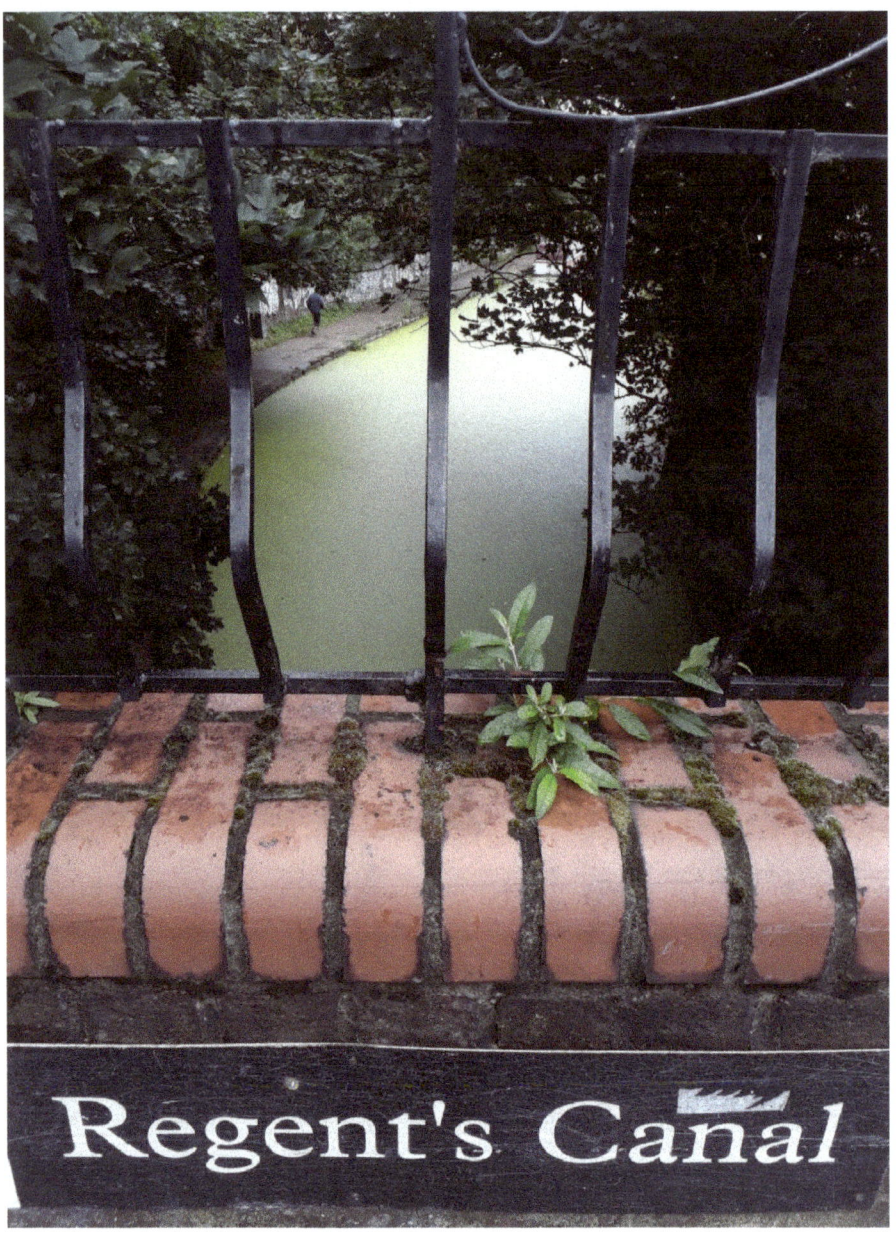

26.7.2017 - 12:51:11

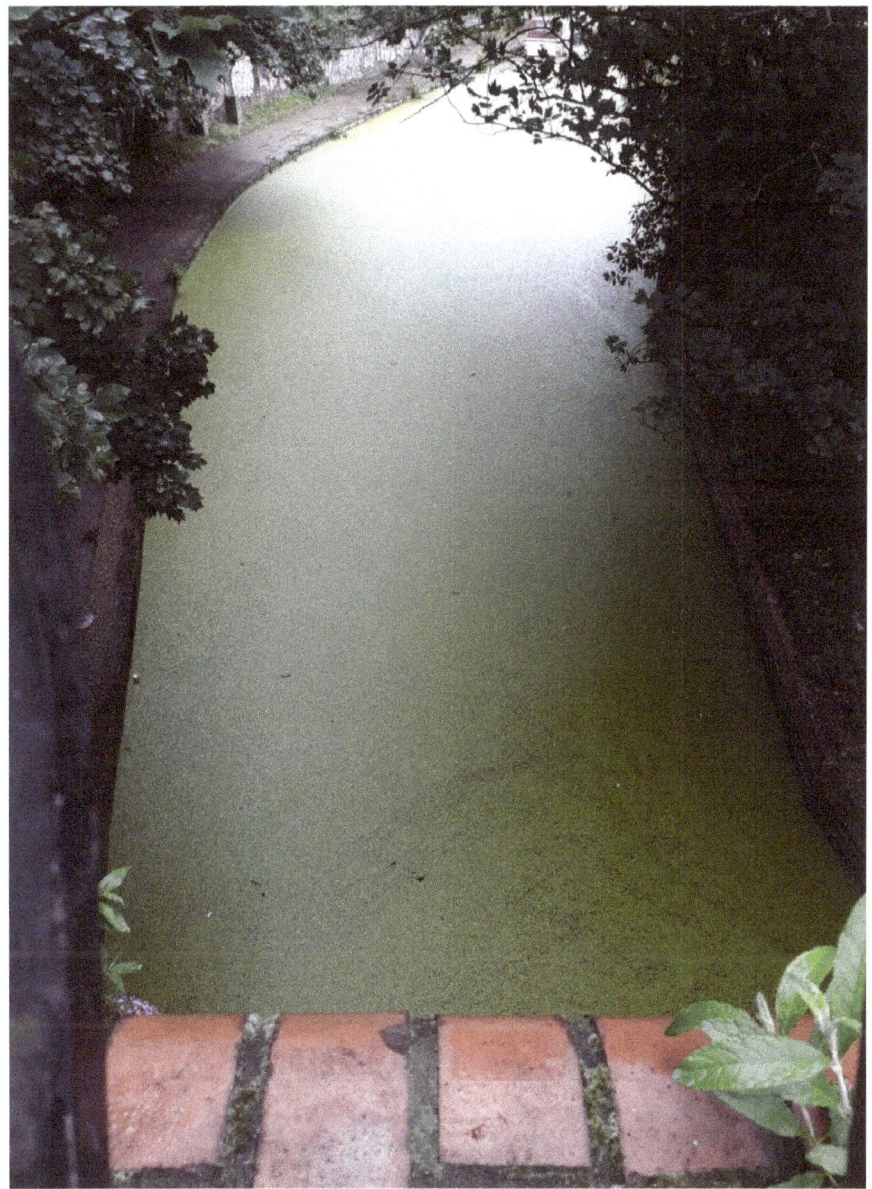

26.7.2017 - 12:51:18

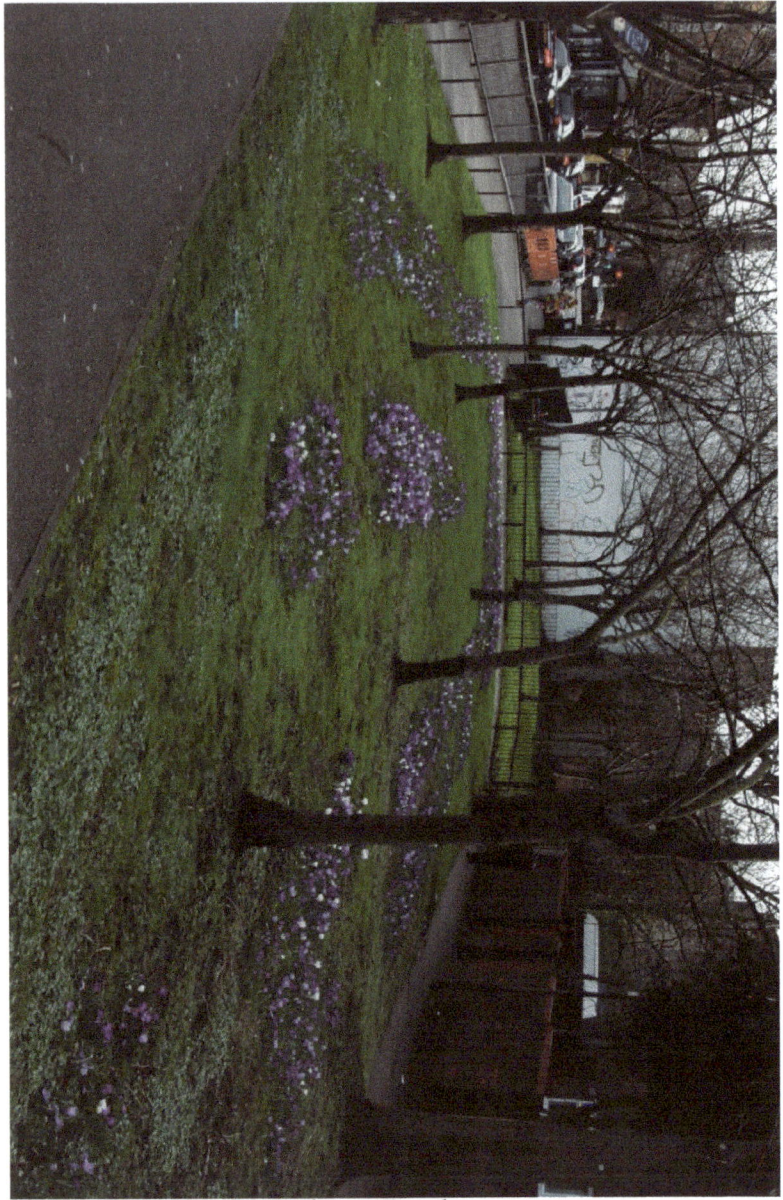

7.3.2004 - 12:41:26, Valance Road

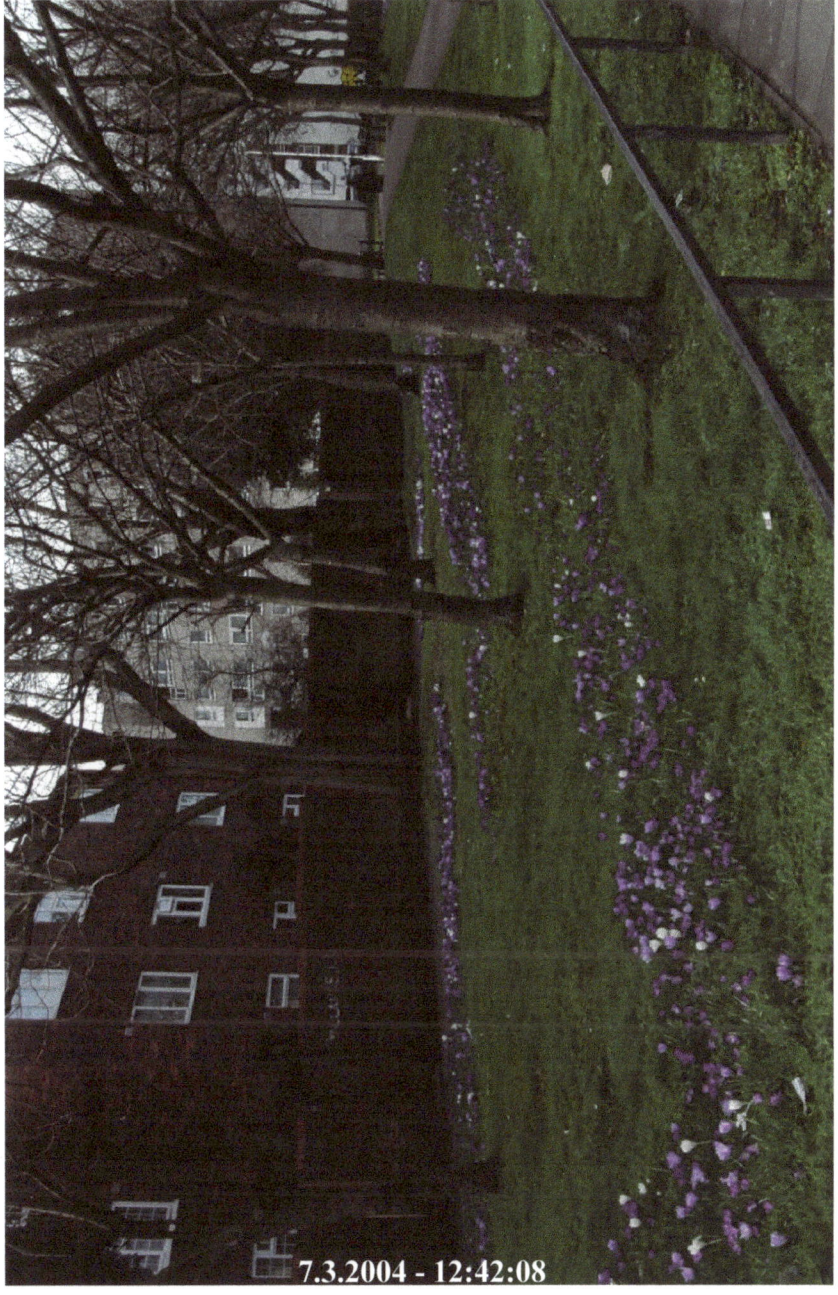

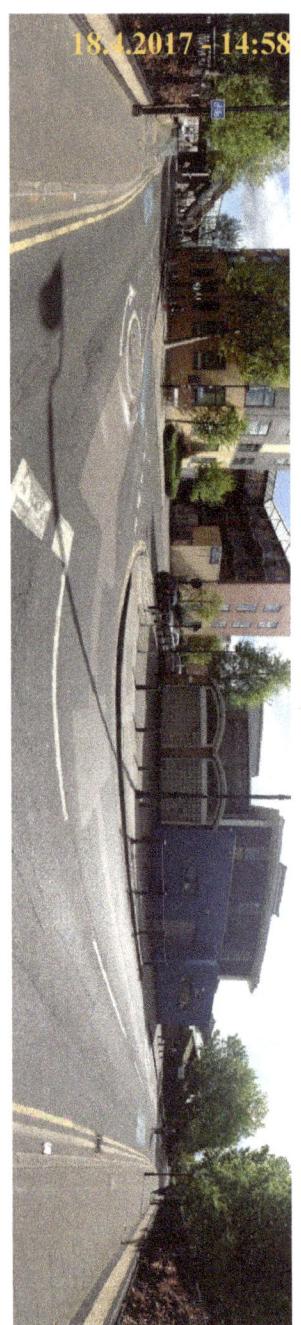 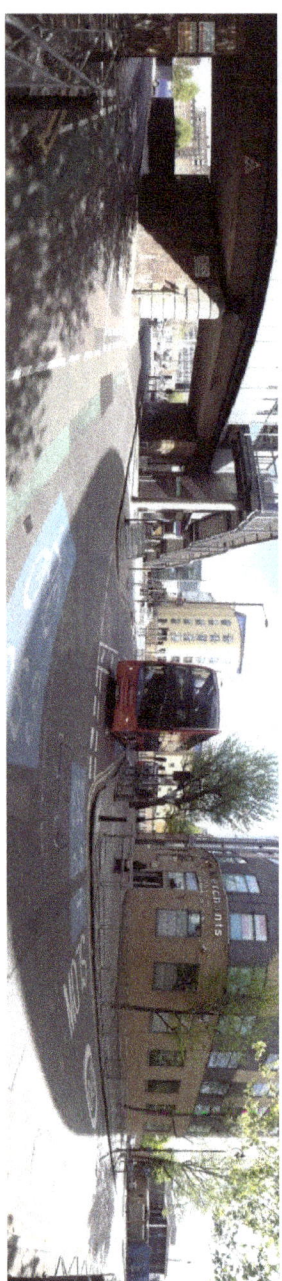 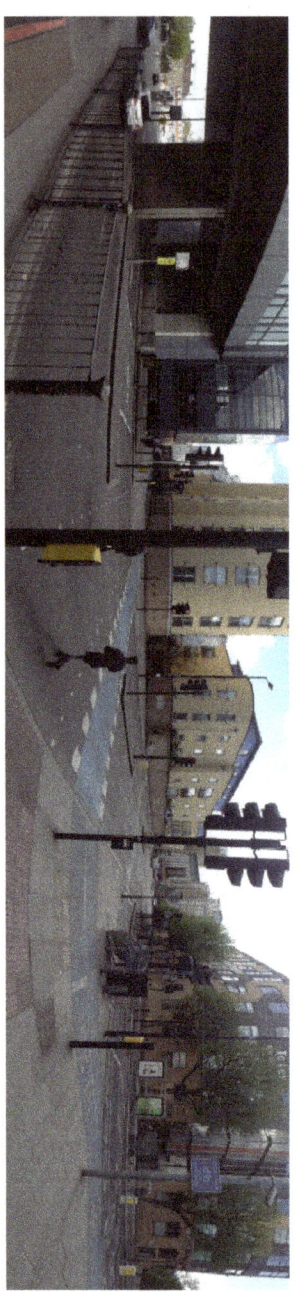

18.4.2017 - 15:07

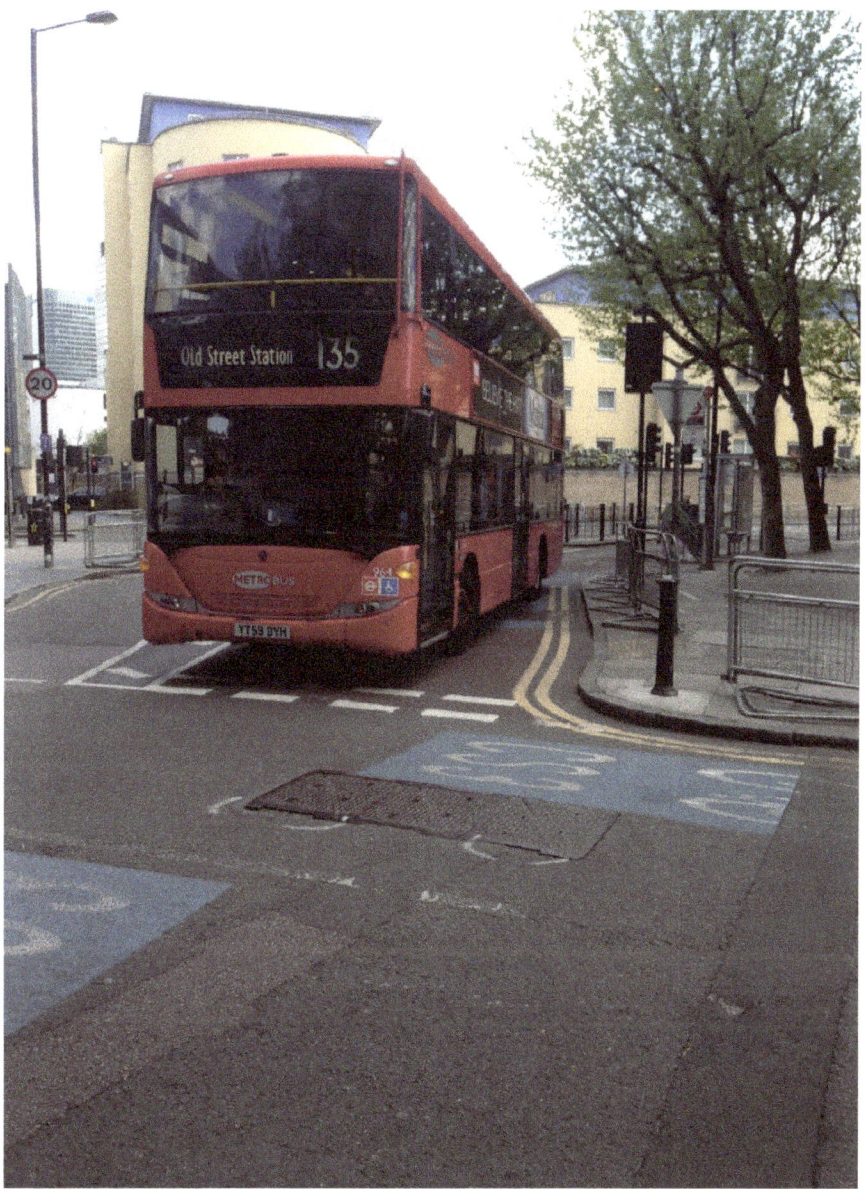

18.4.2017 - 15:01, Salter Street view

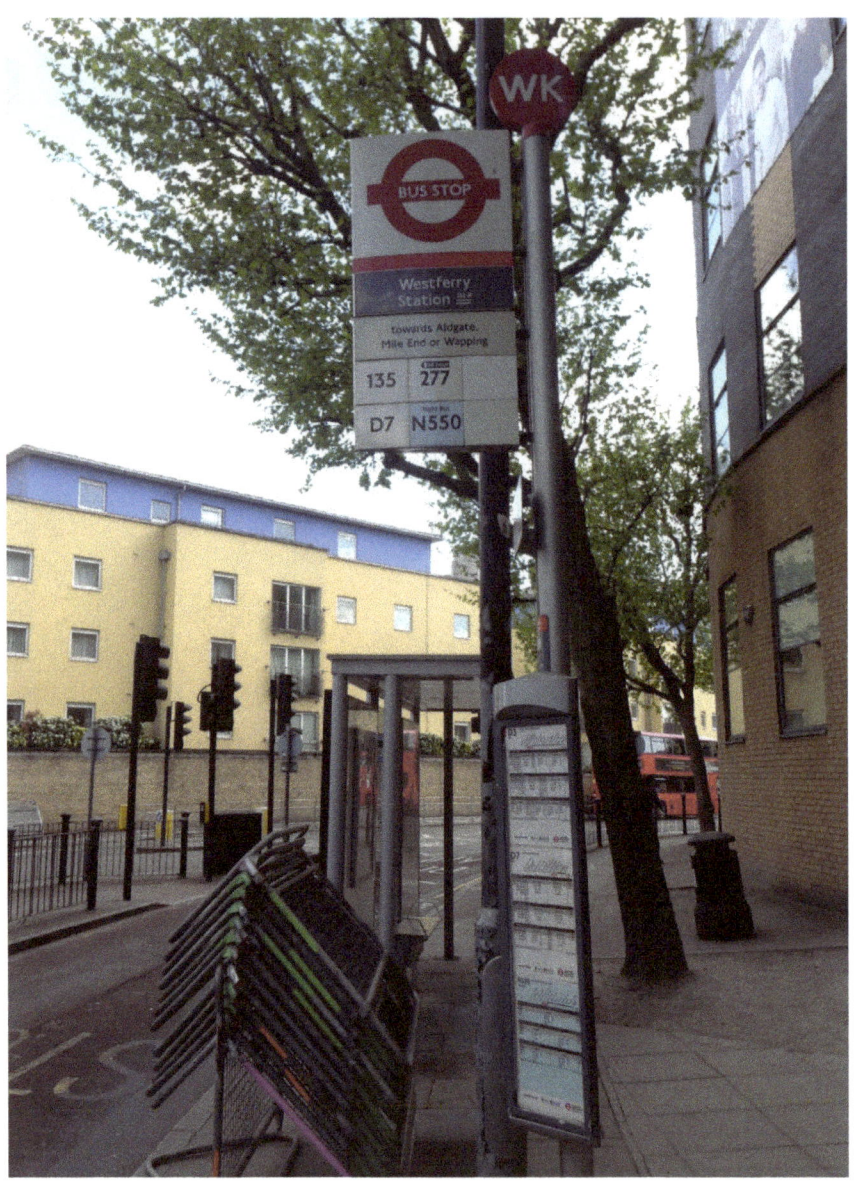

18.4.2017 - 15:02

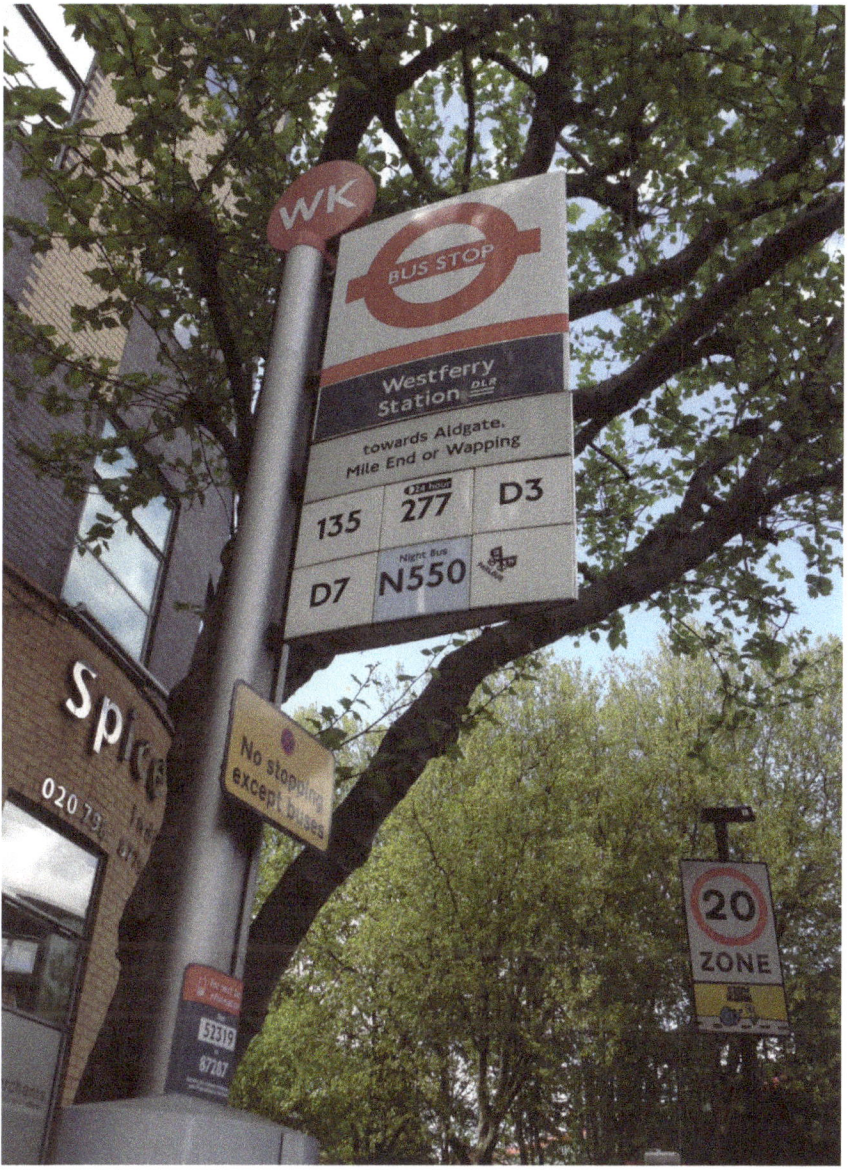

18.4.2017 - 15:03

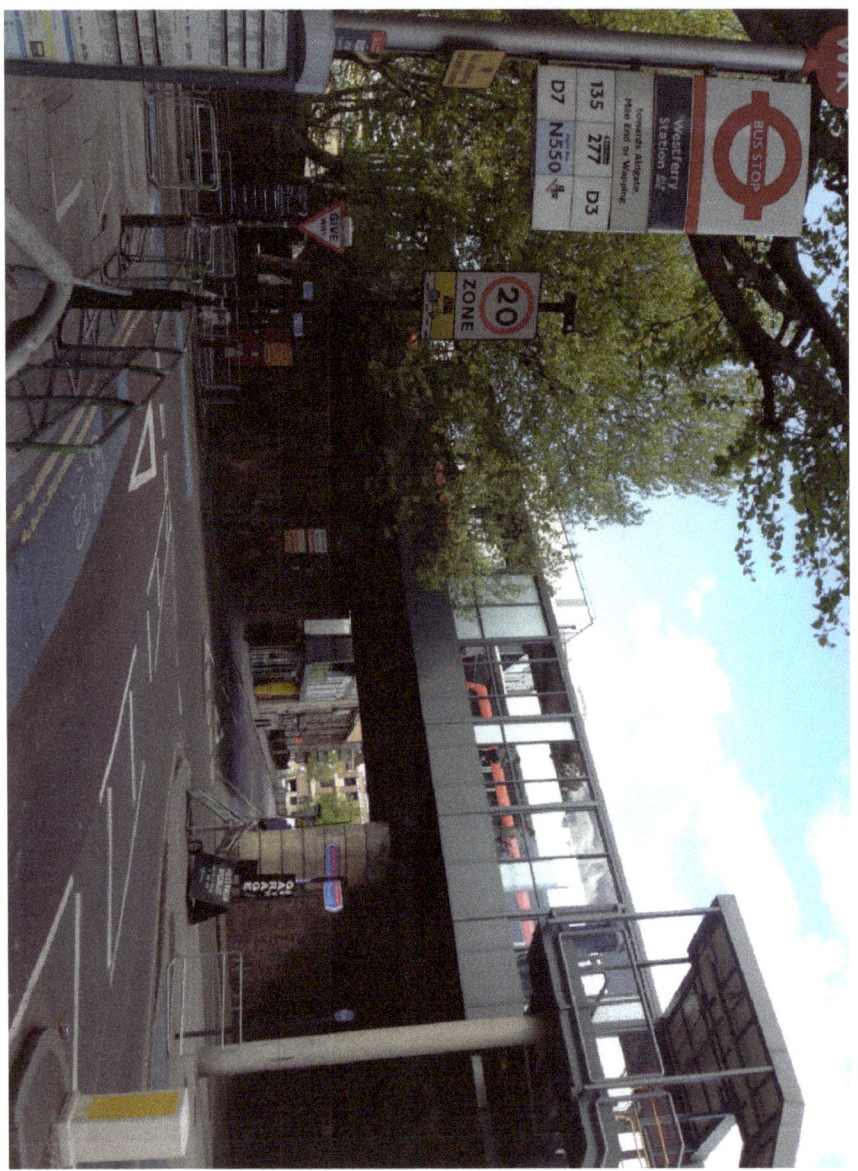

18.4.2017 - 15:03

East End Photos, Through Mayar's Eyes : **Tower Hamlets, Random One**

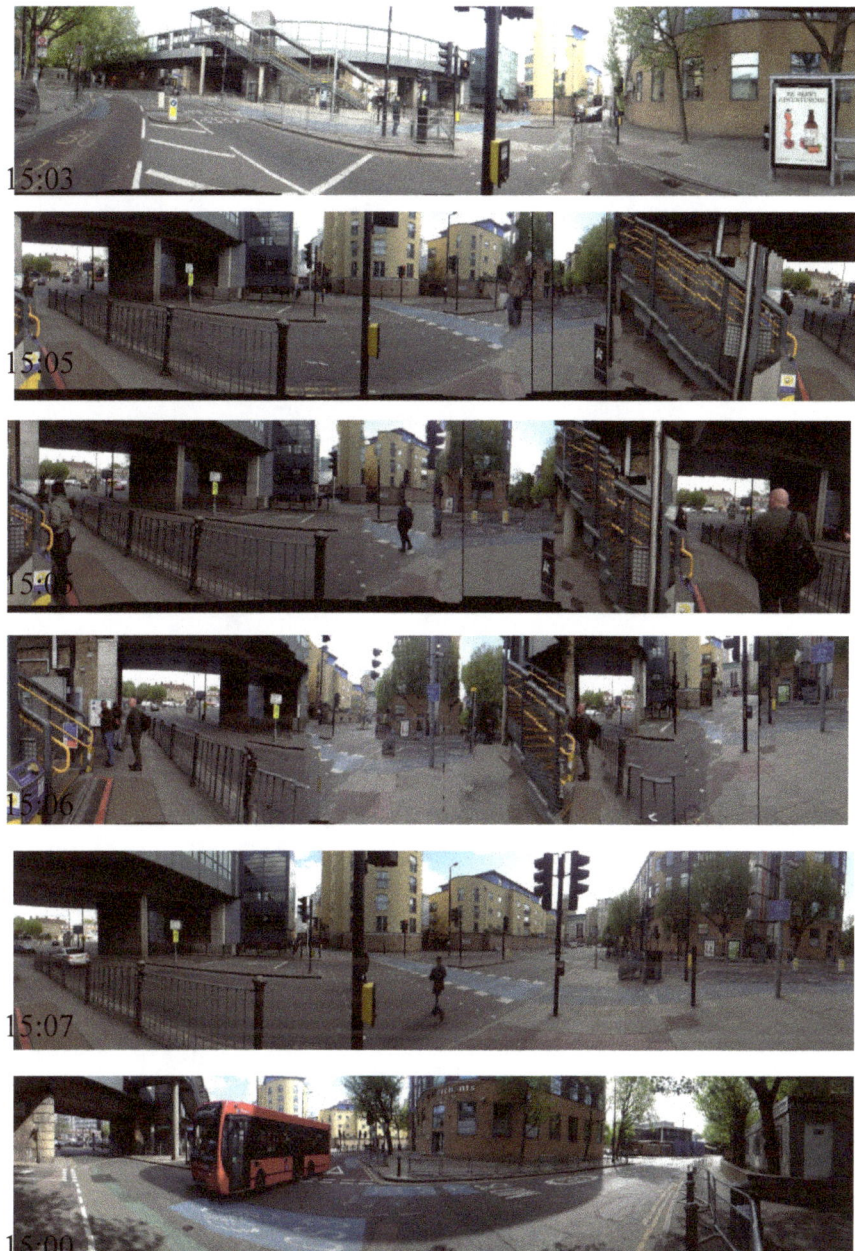

**18.4.2017**

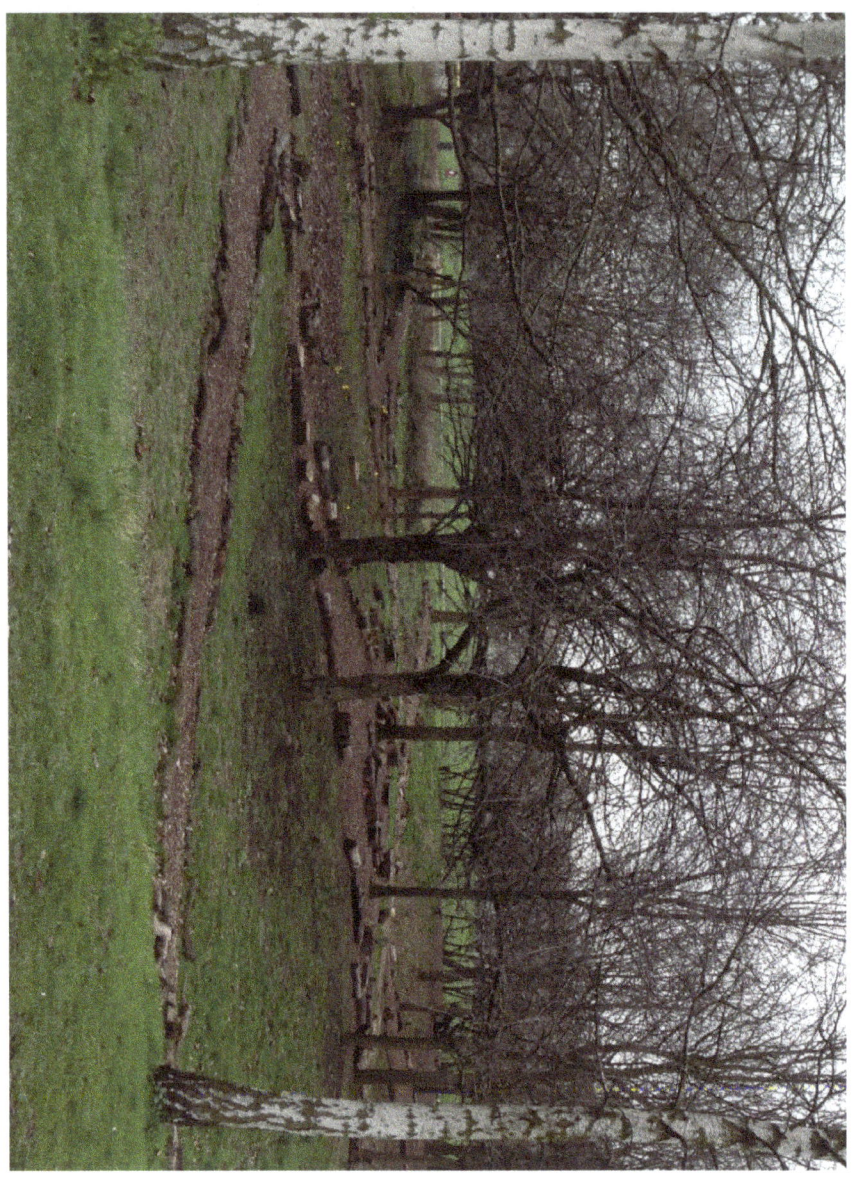

1.3.2017 - 17:18:19, Mile End Park, Burdett Road

East End Photos, Through Mayar's Eyes : **Tower Hamlets, Random One**

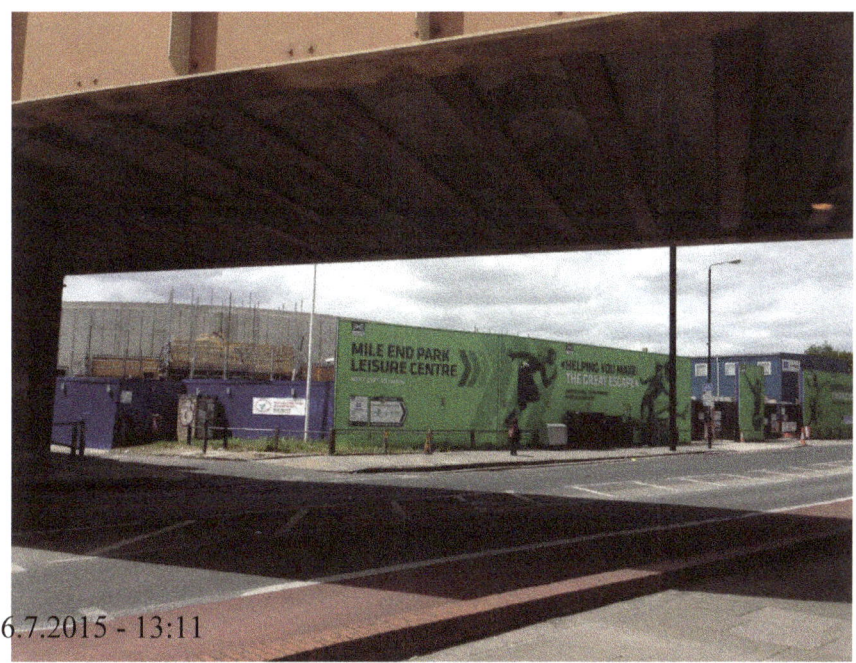

6.7.2015 - 13:11

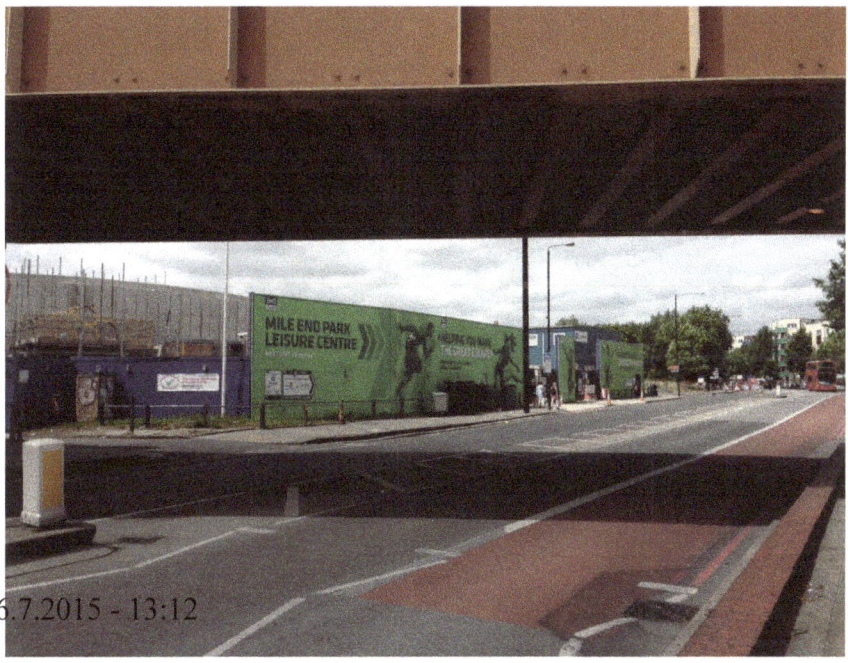

6.7.2015 - 13:12

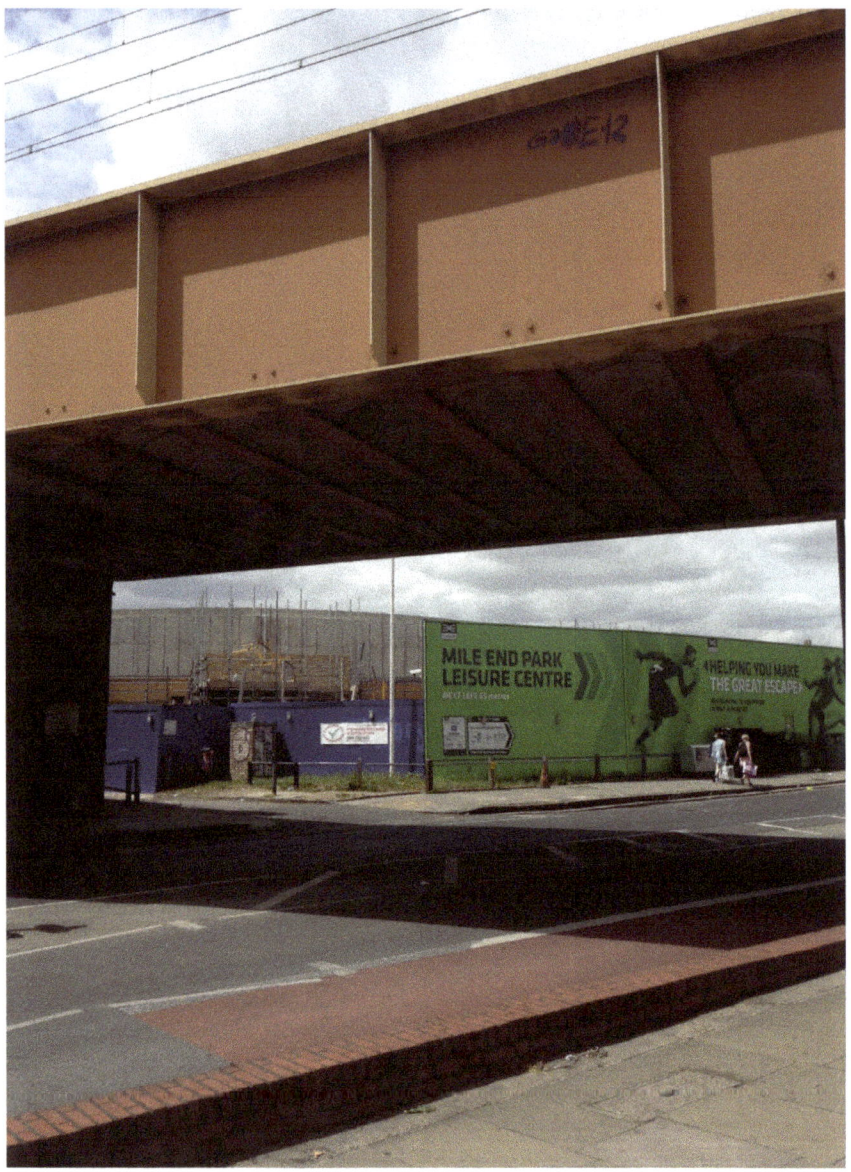

6.7.2015 - 13:11, Burdett Road, looking towards the leisure centre

East End Photos, Through Mayar's Eyes : **Tower Hamlets, Random One**

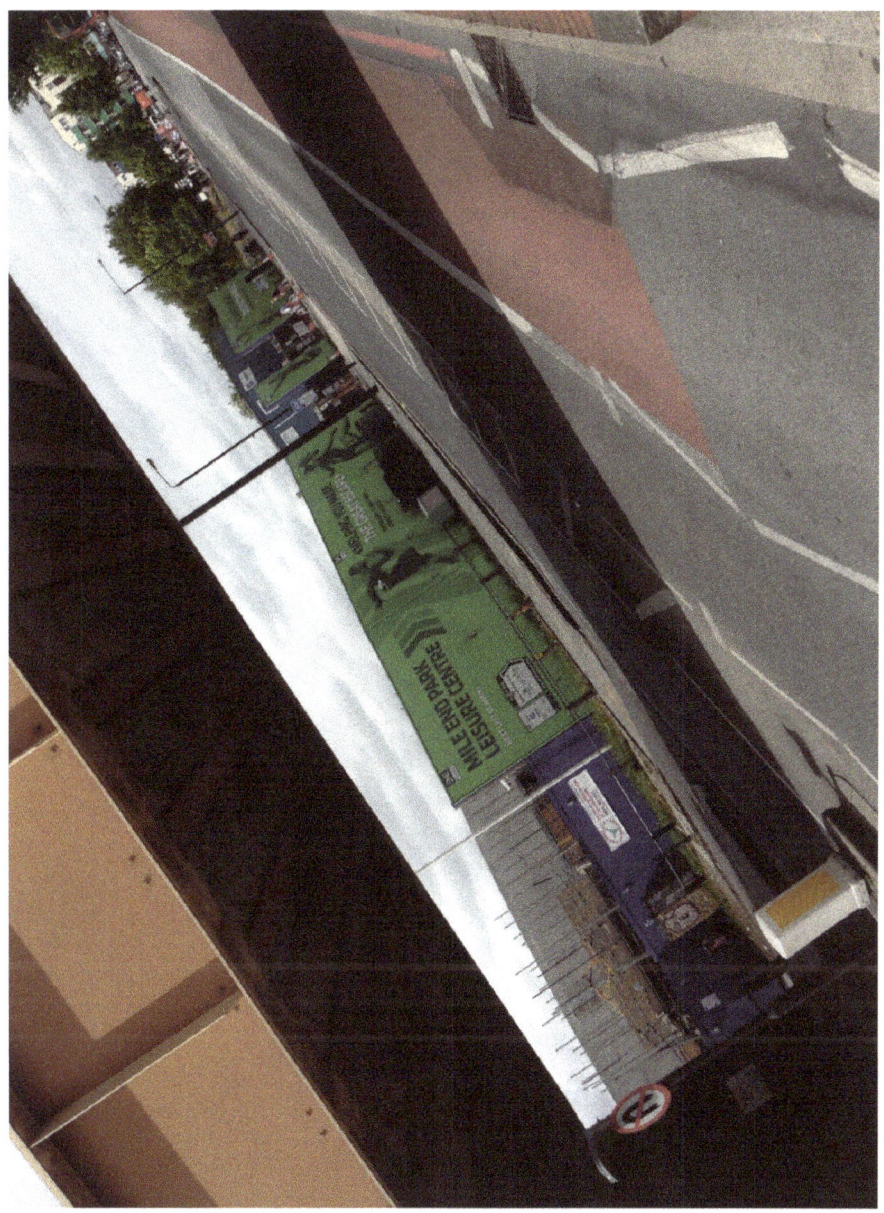

6.7.2015 - 13:12

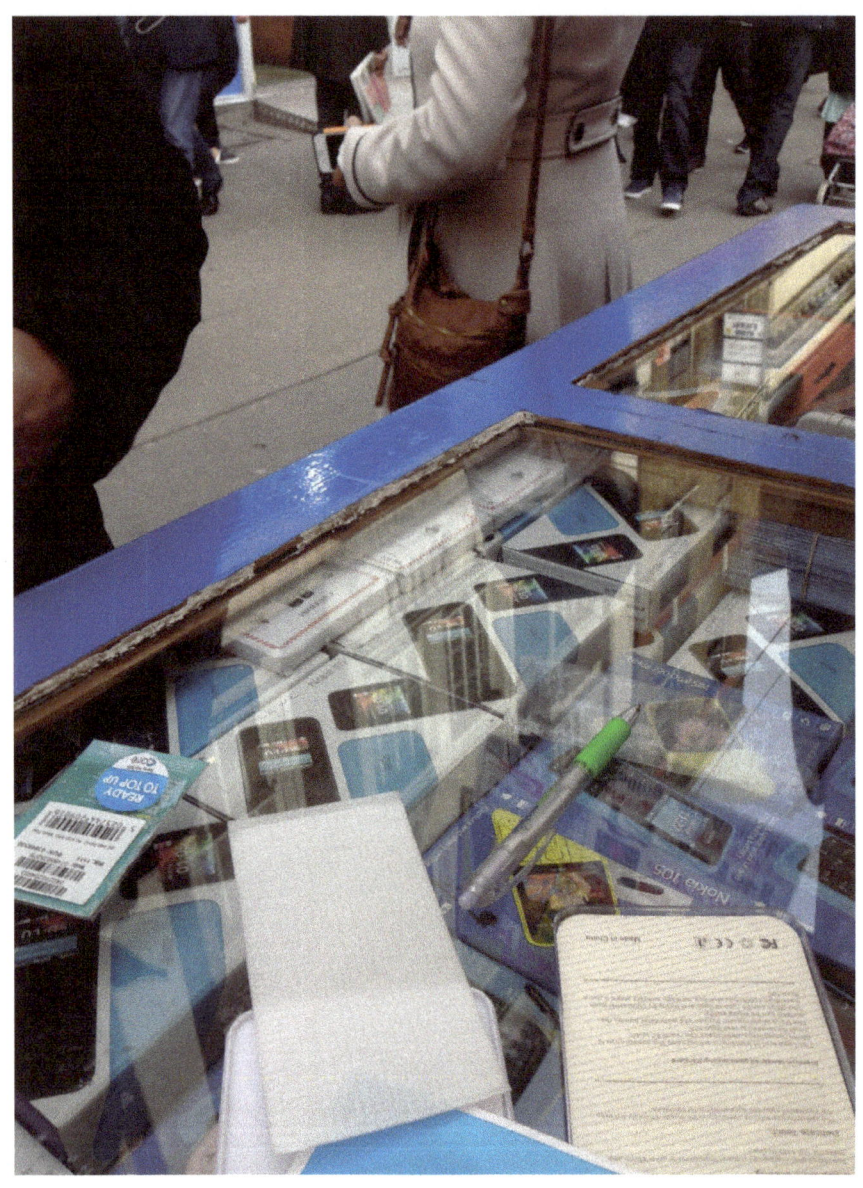

13.1.2016 - 12:33, Whitechapel Market

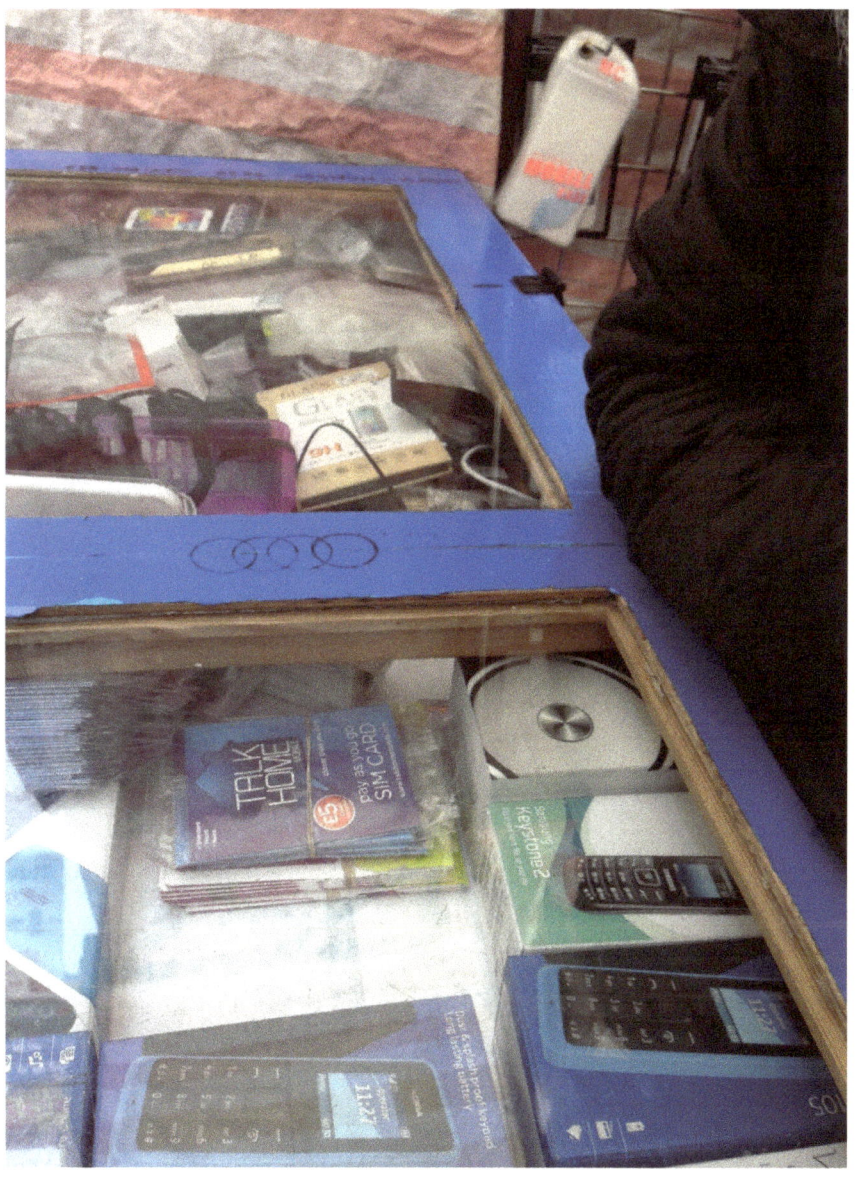

13.1.2016 - 12:33

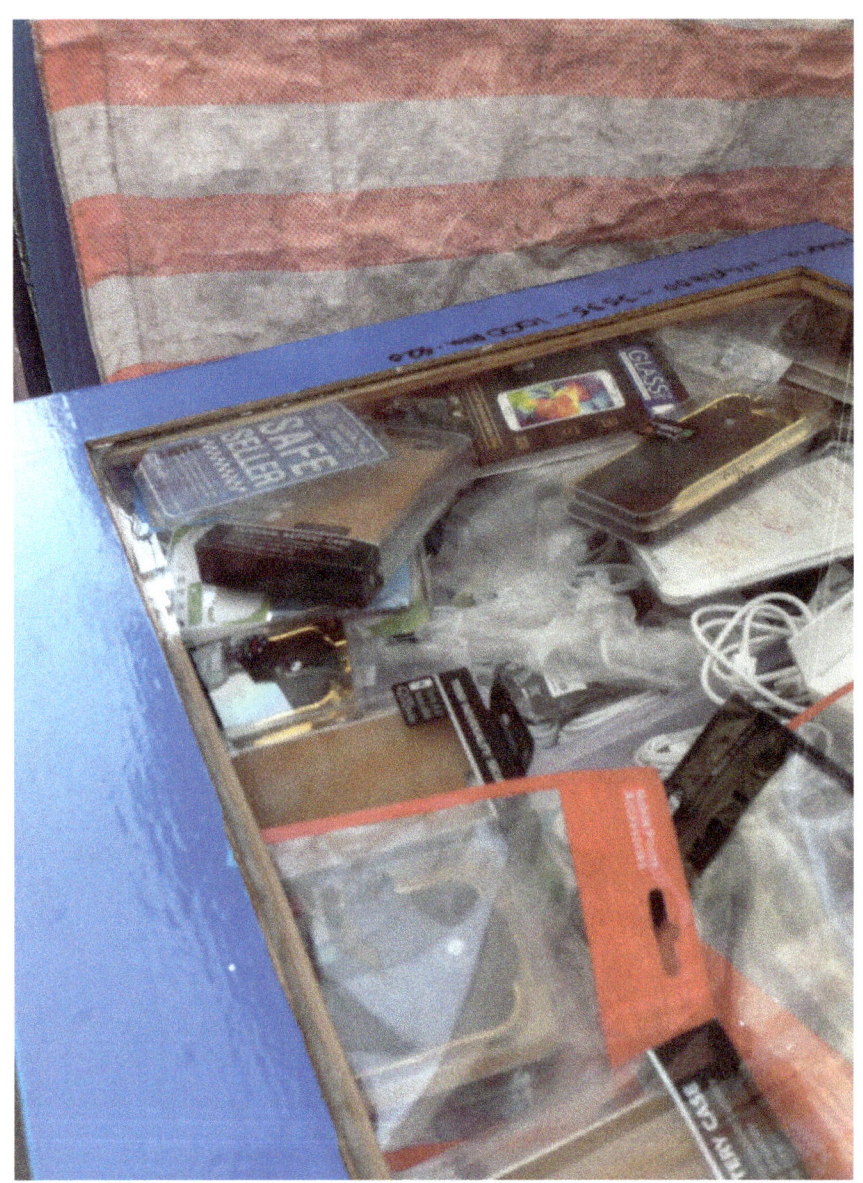

13.1.2016 - 13:00

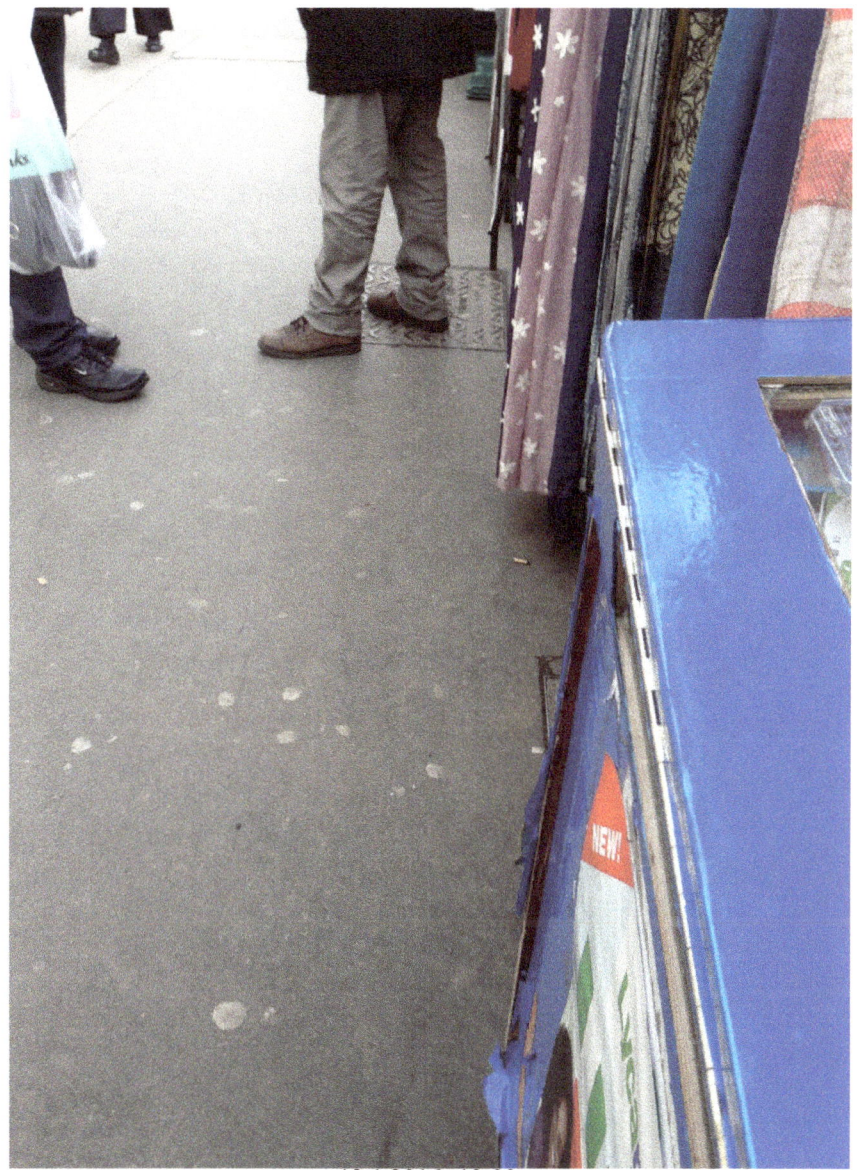

13.1.2016 -13:00

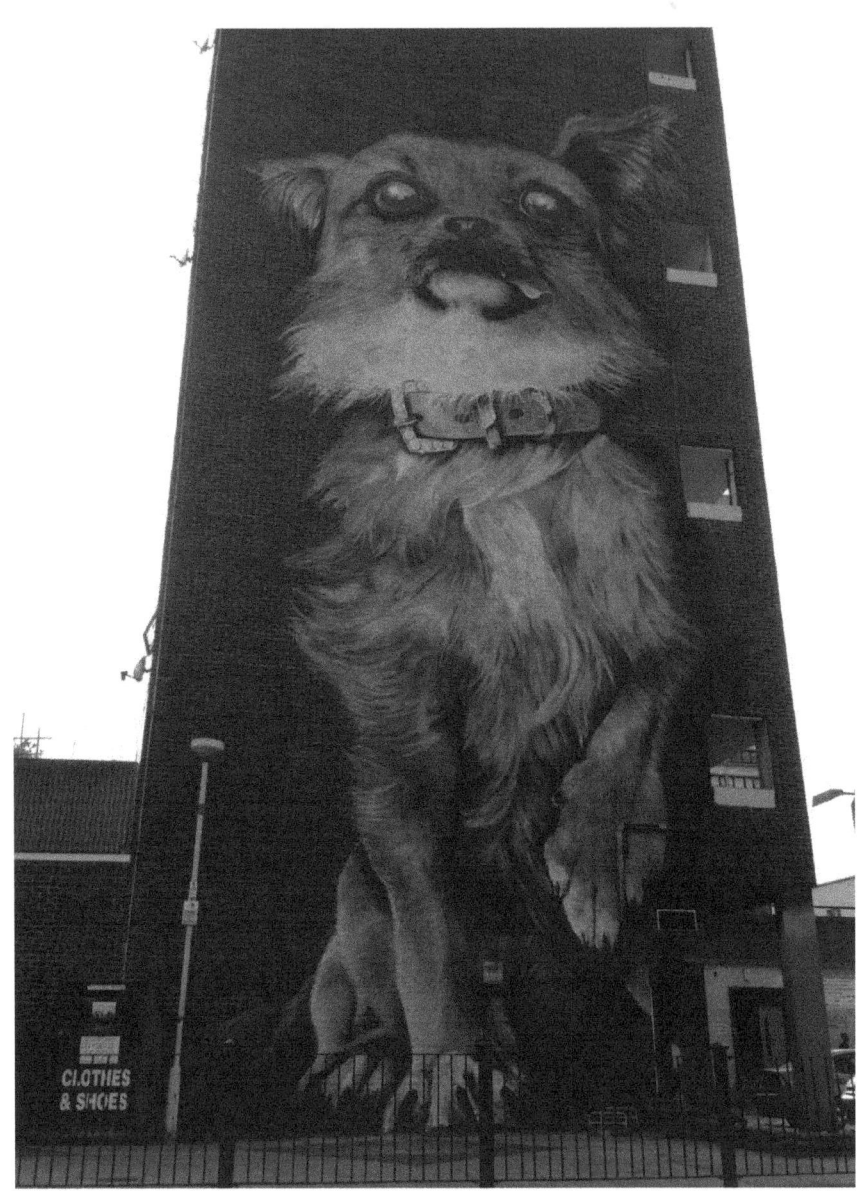

1.7.2015 - 17:06, Crisp Street, Poplar

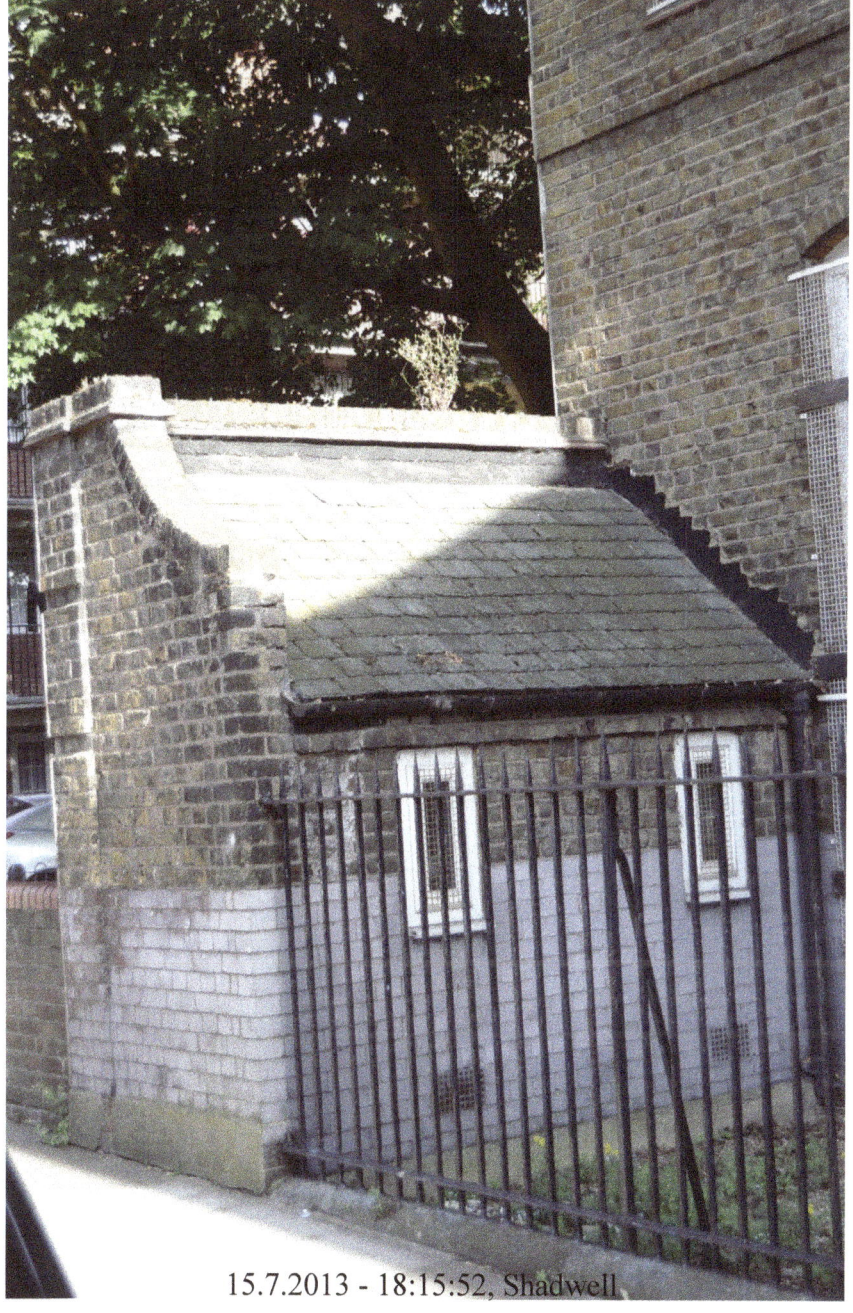

15.7.2013 - 18:15:52, Shadwell

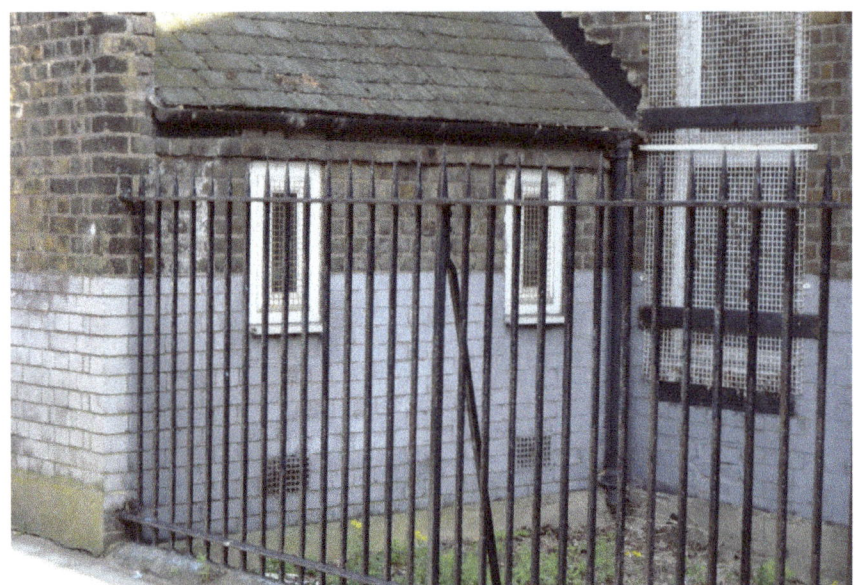

15.7.2013 - 18:16:02, Shadwell

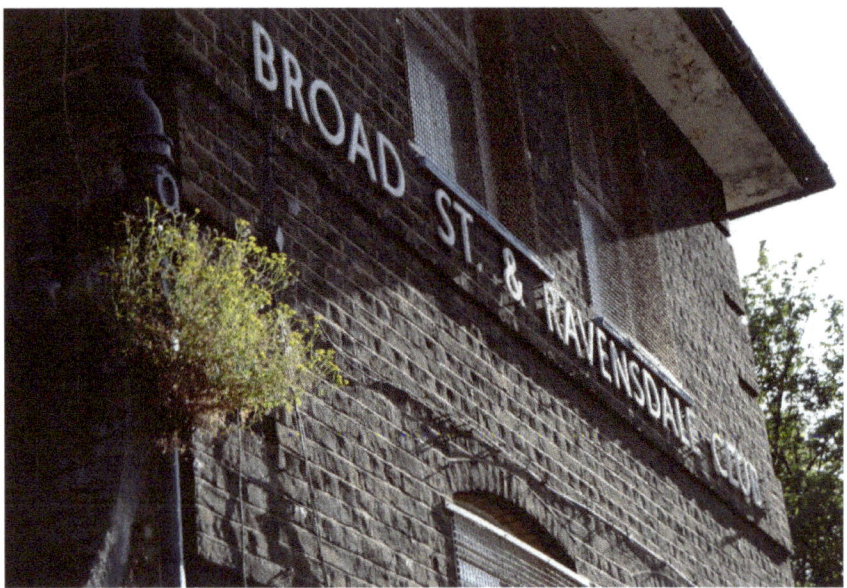

15.7.2013 - 18:30:12, Shadwell

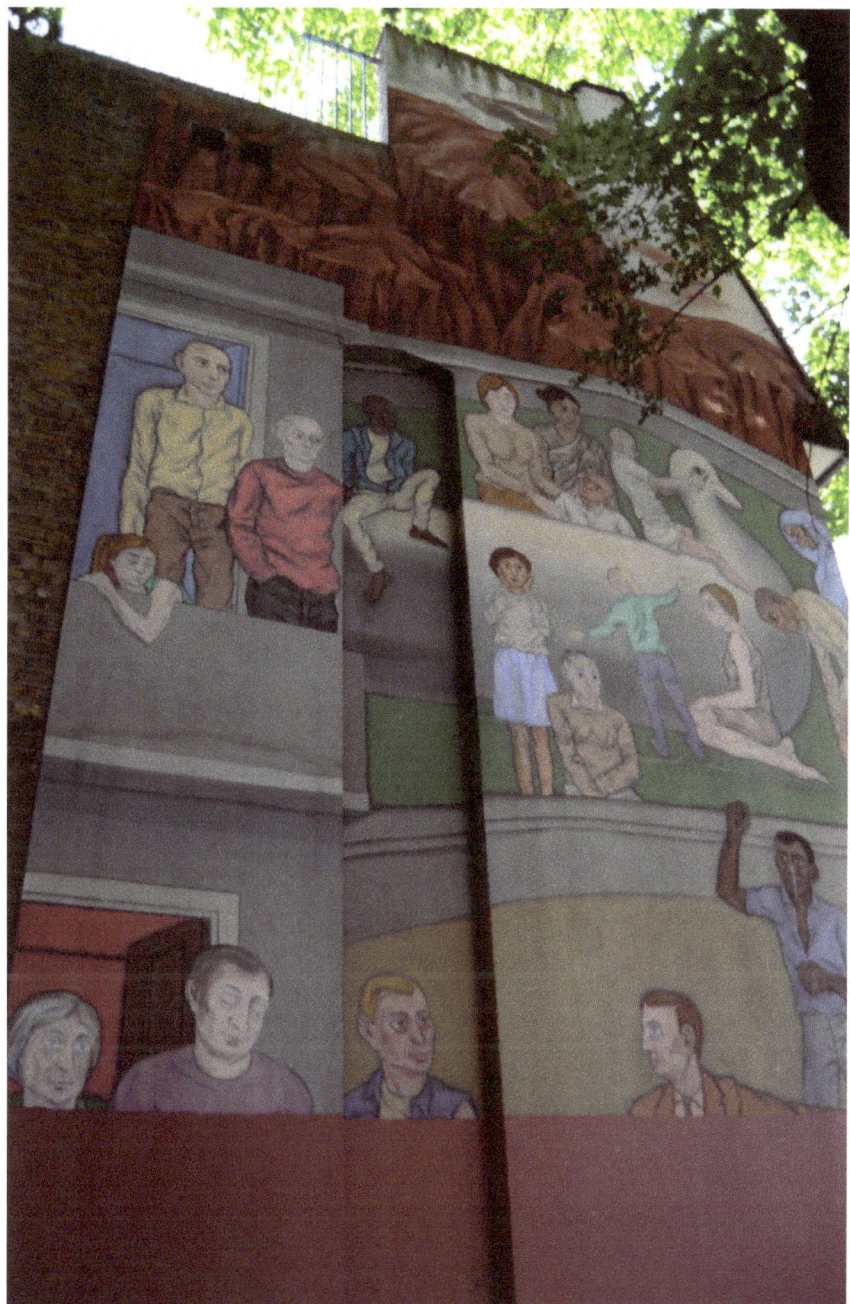

15.7.2013 - 18:15:52, Shadwell

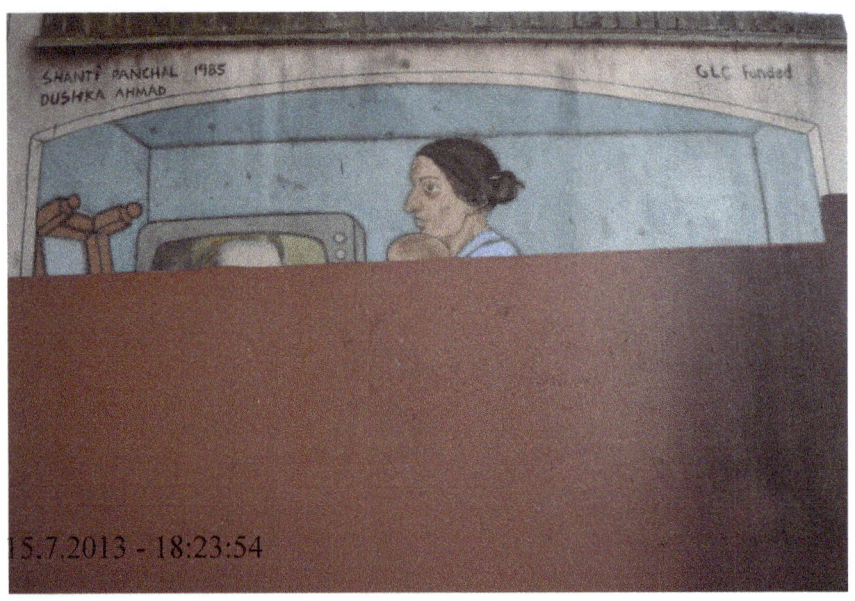

15.7.2013 - 18:23:54

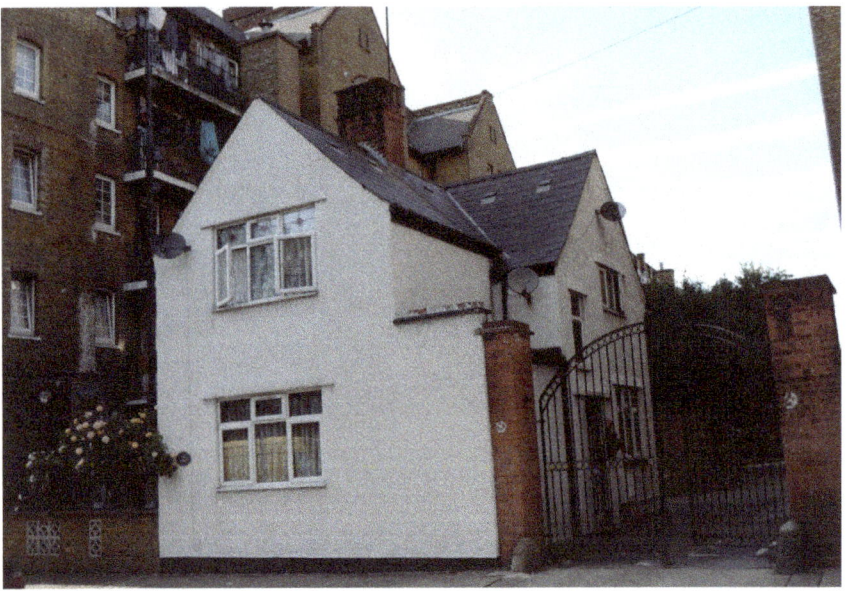

15.7.2013 - 18:29:28, Shadwell

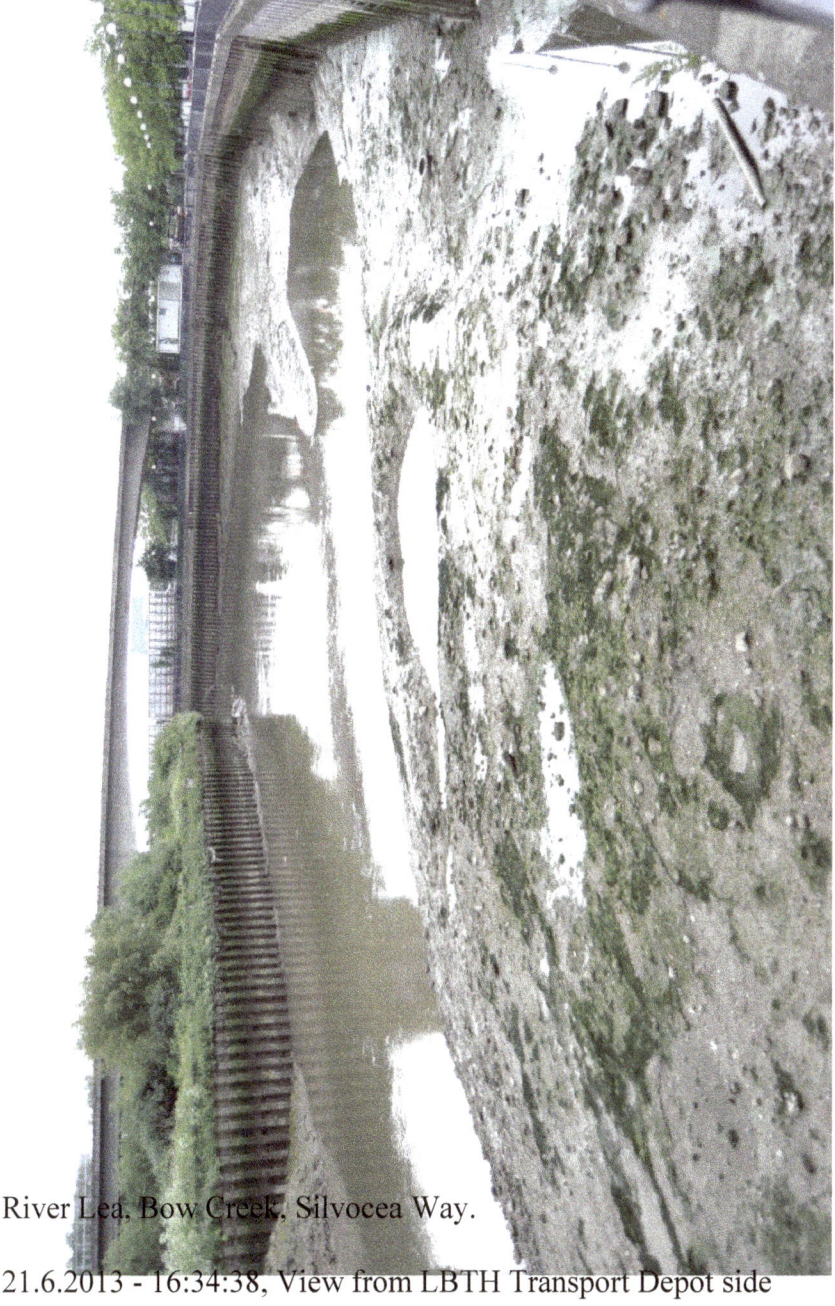

River Lea, Bow Creek, Silvocea Way.

21.6.2013 - 16:34:38, View from LBTH Transport Depot side

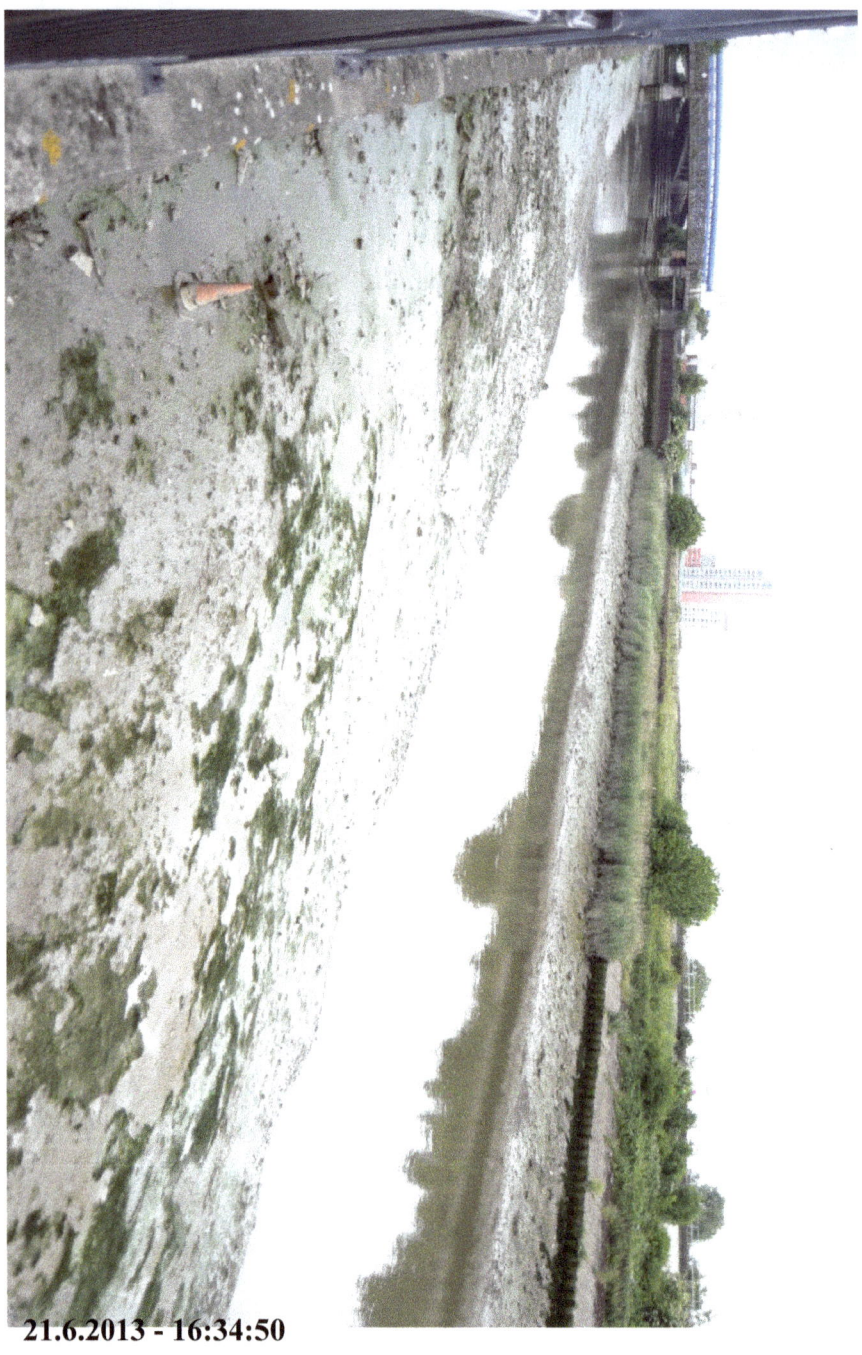

21.6.2013 - 16:34:50

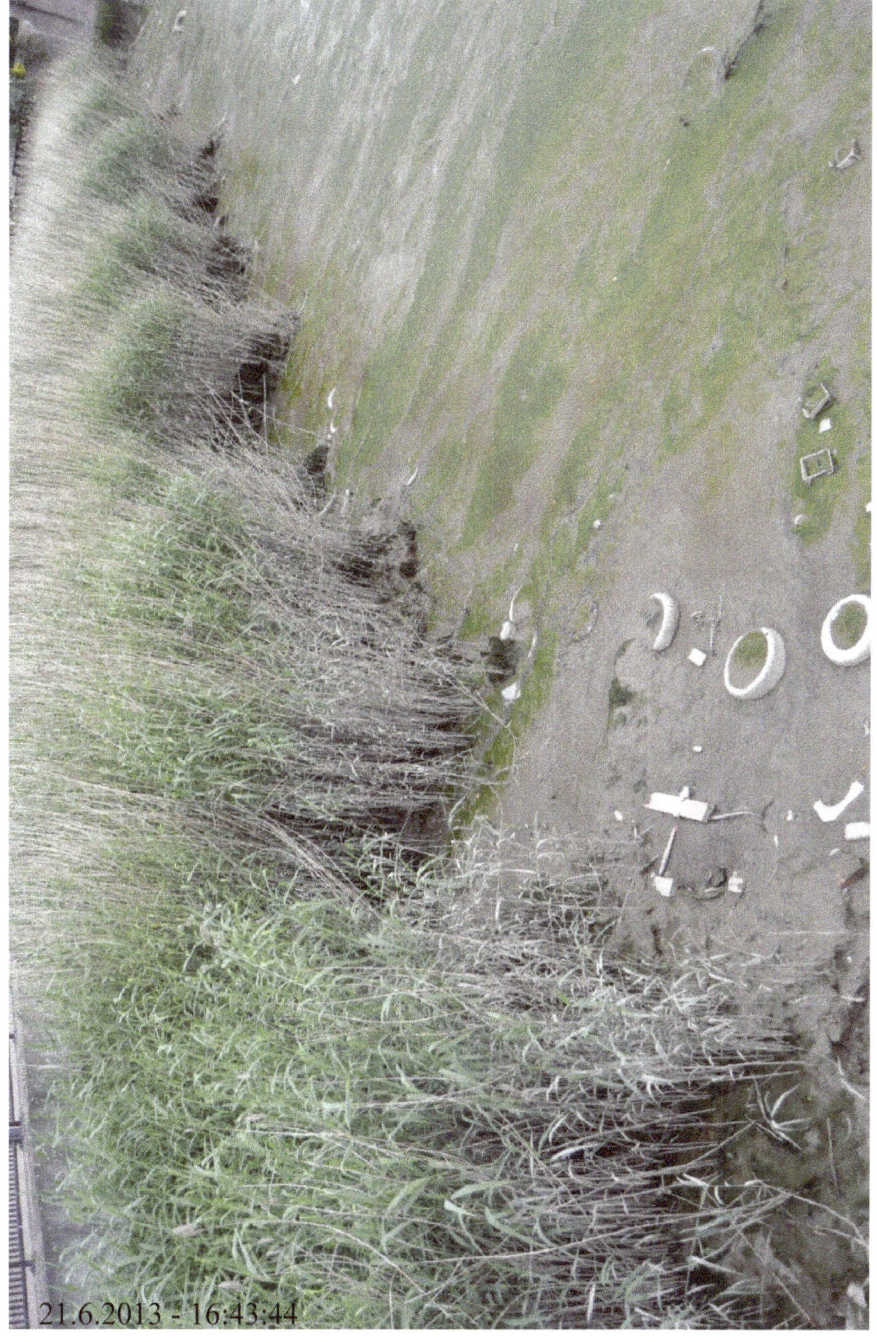

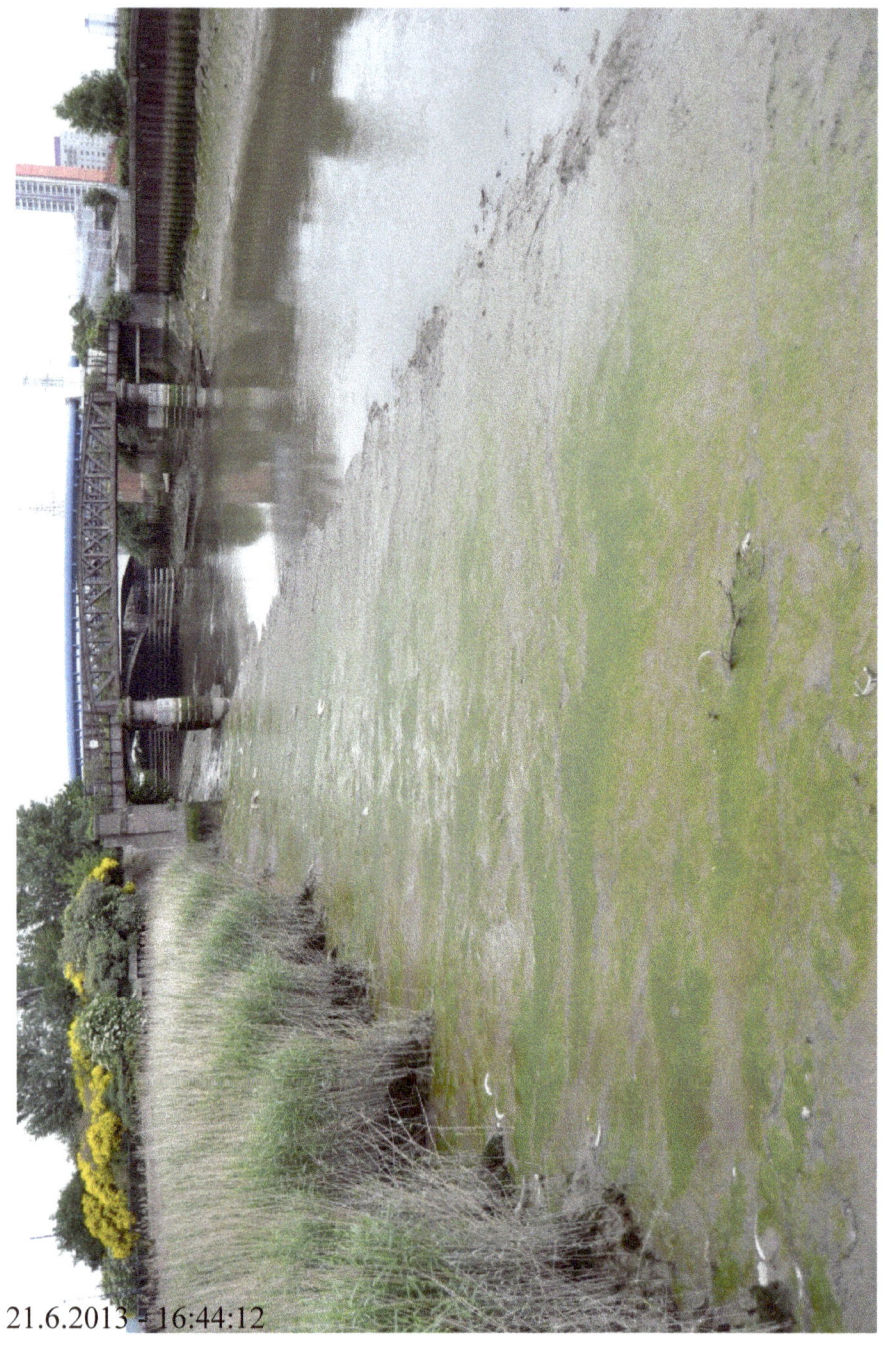

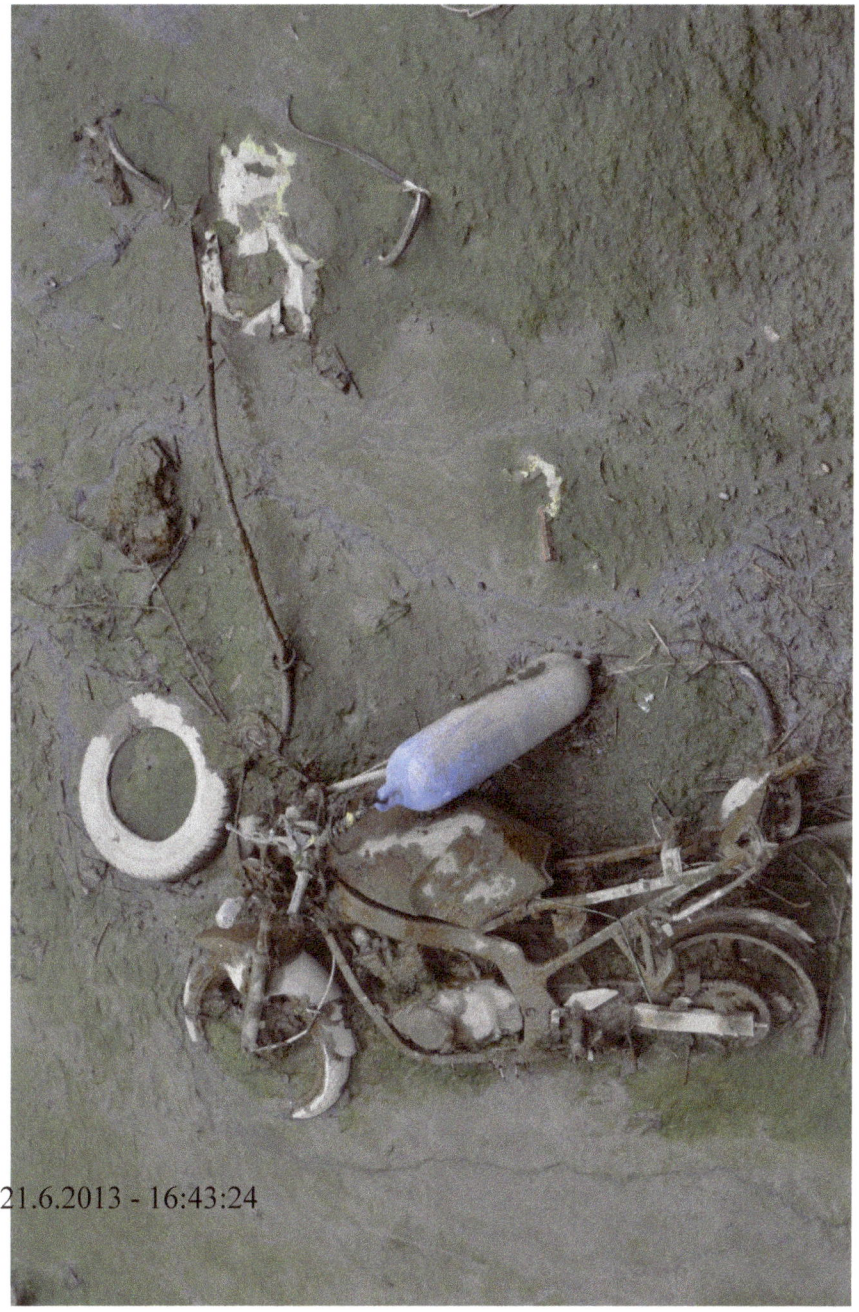

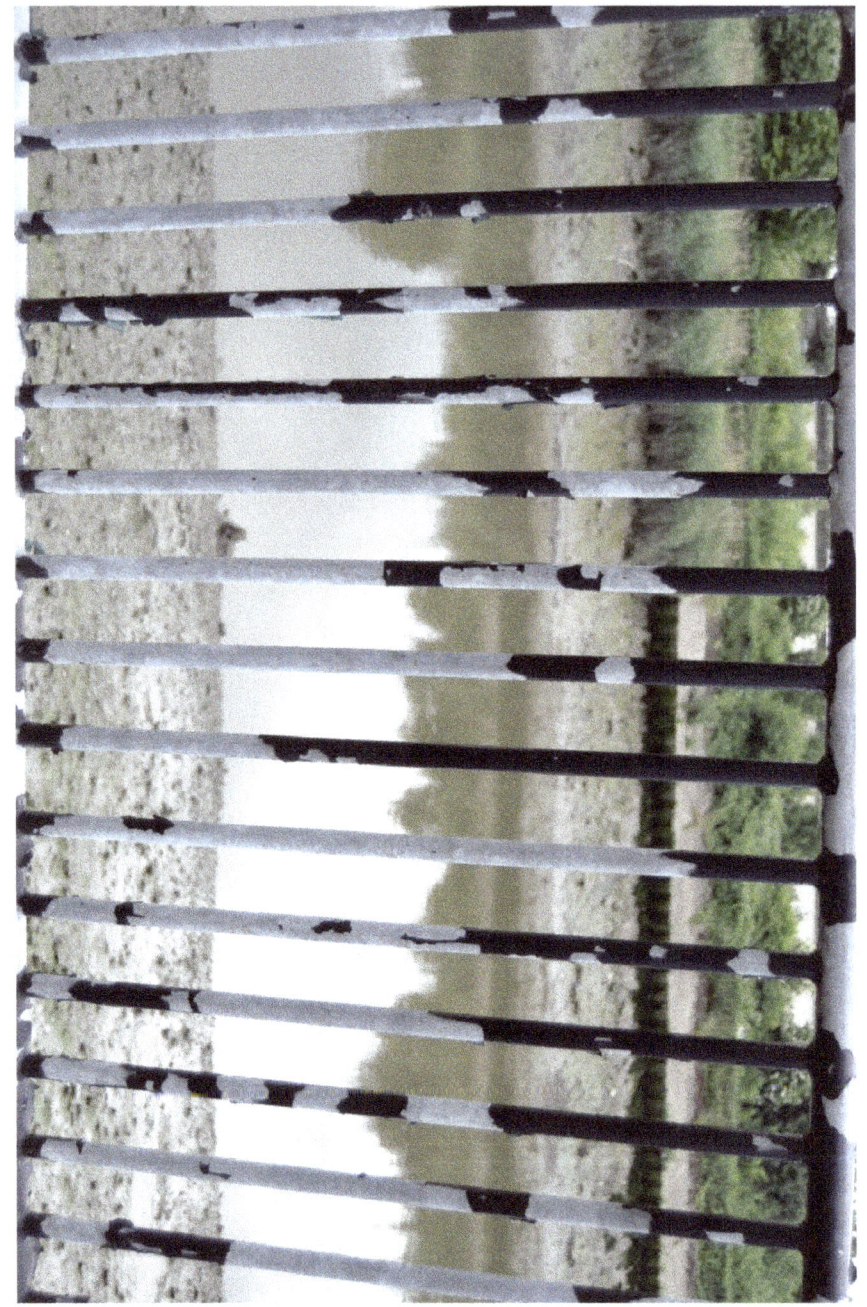

21.6.2013 - 16:40:20

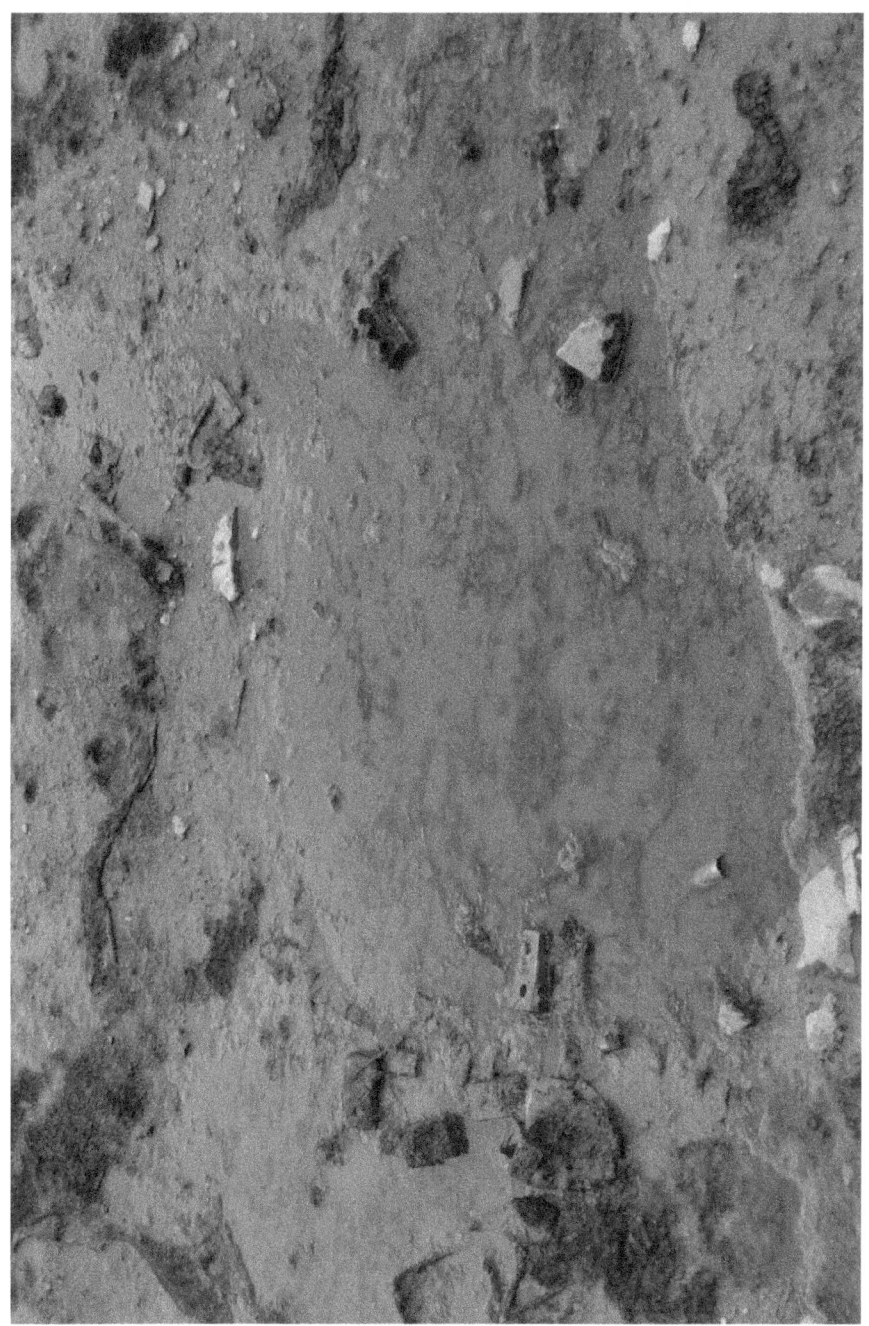

21.6.2013 - 16:435:12

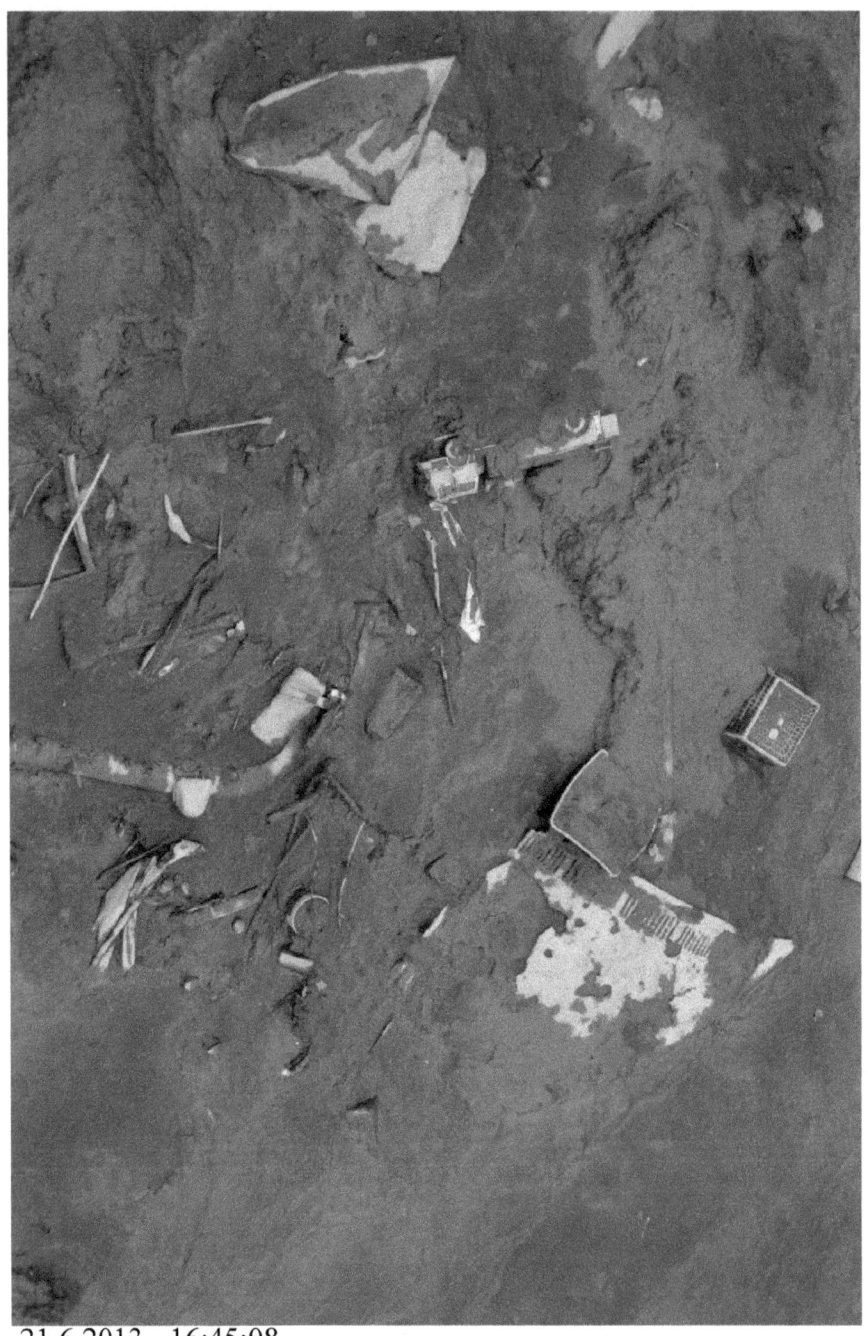

21.6.2013 - 16:45:08

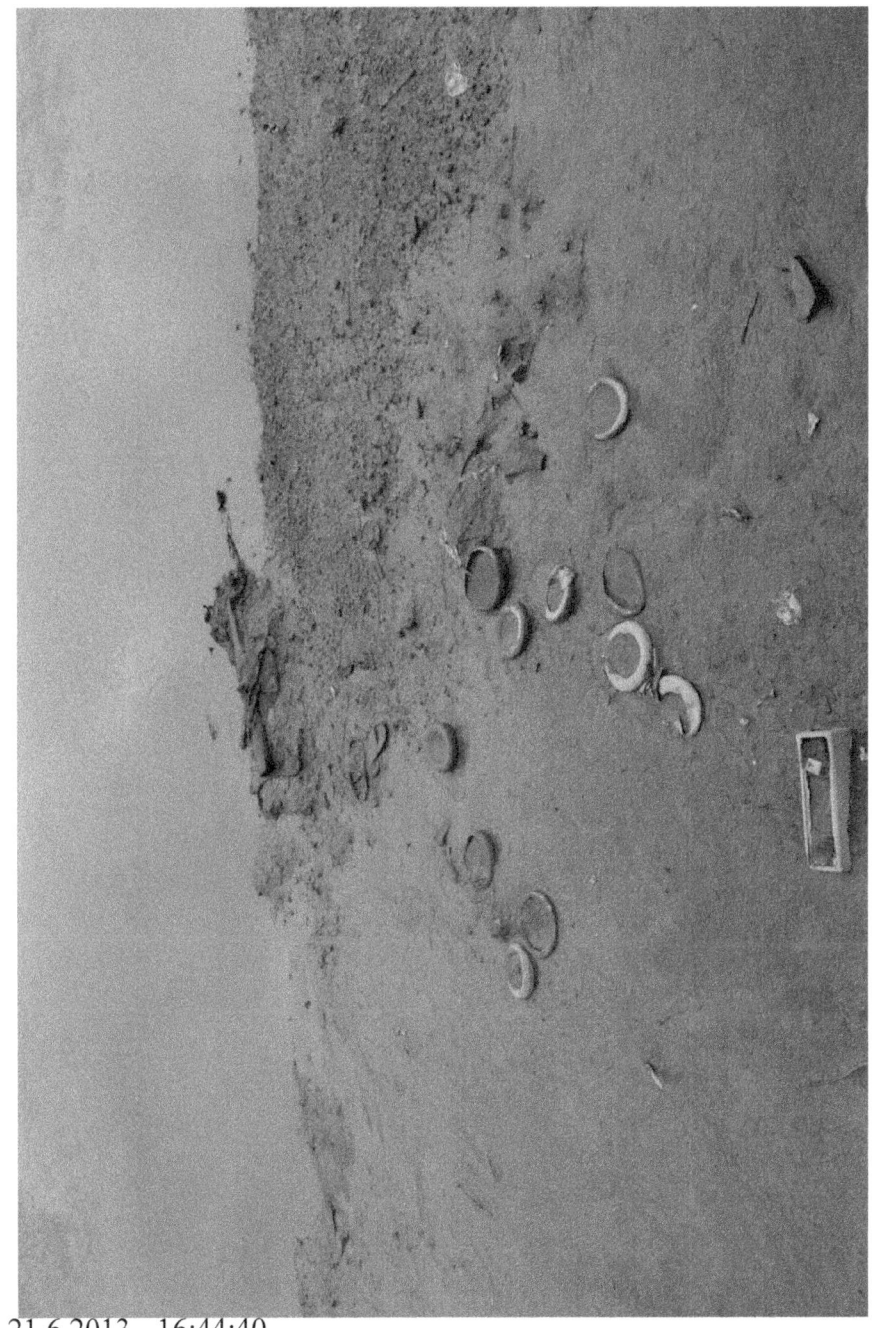

21.6.2013 - 16:44:40

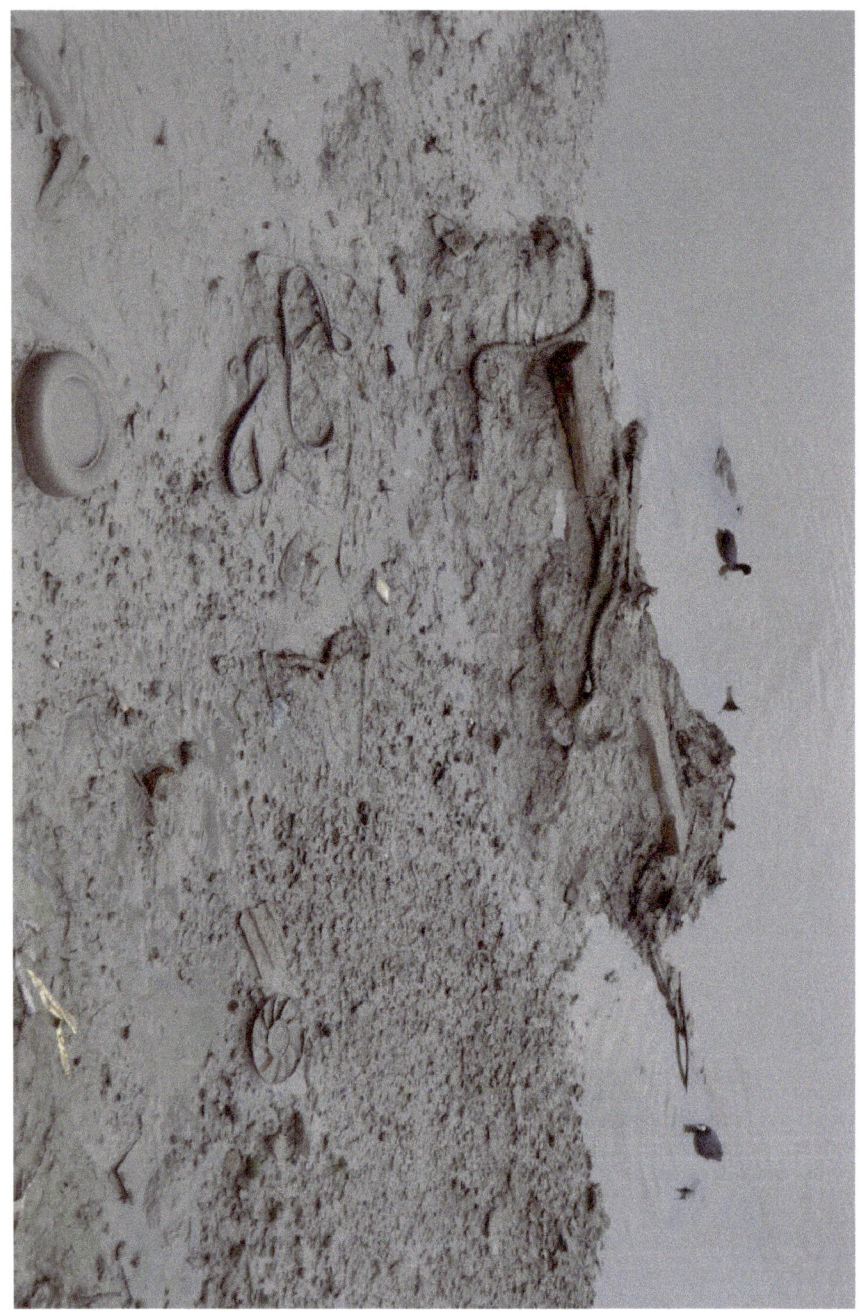
21.6.2013 - 16:44:28

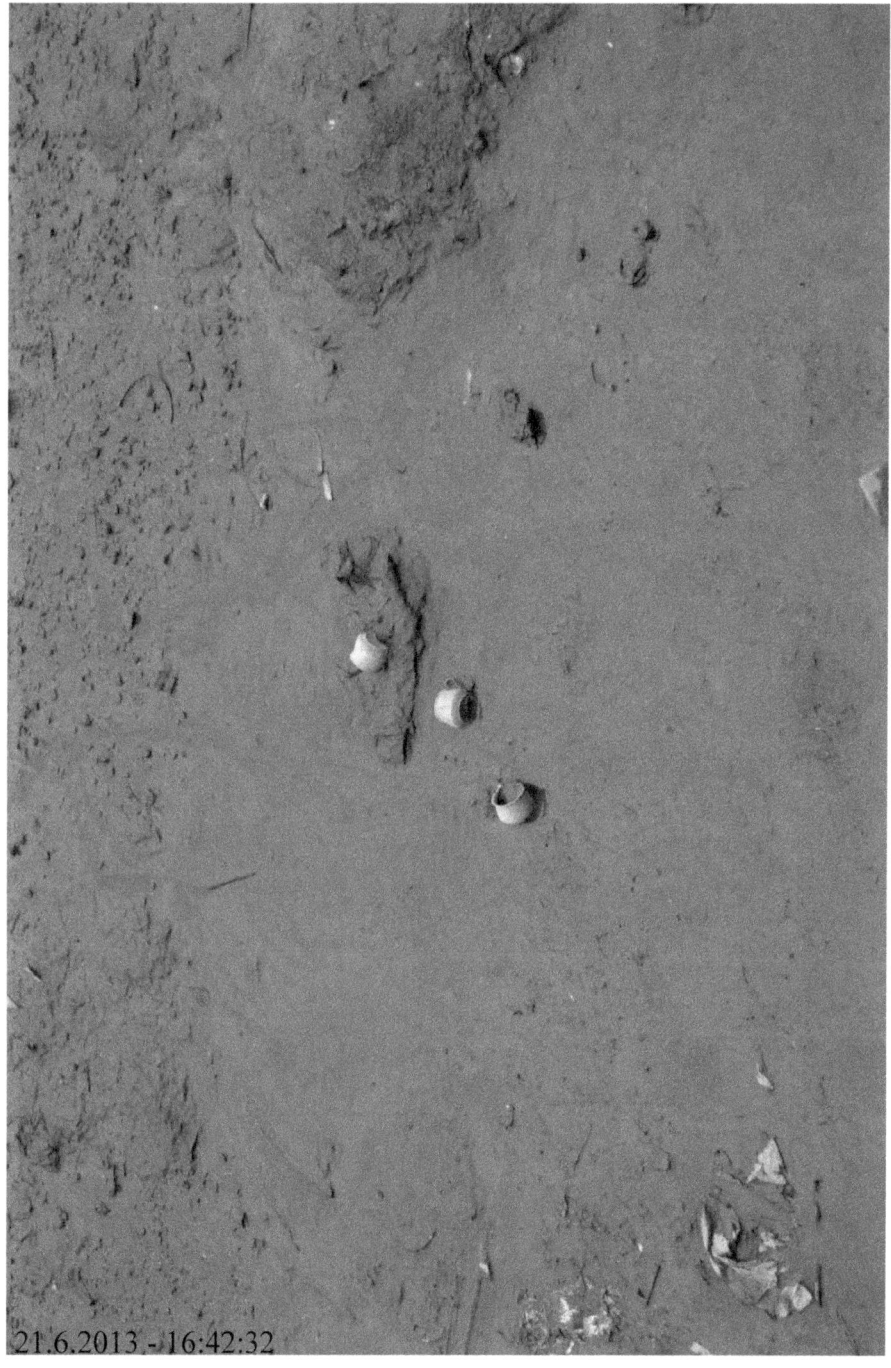

11.7.2013 - 17:24:34

East End Photos, Through Mayar's Eyes : **Tower Hamlets, Random One**

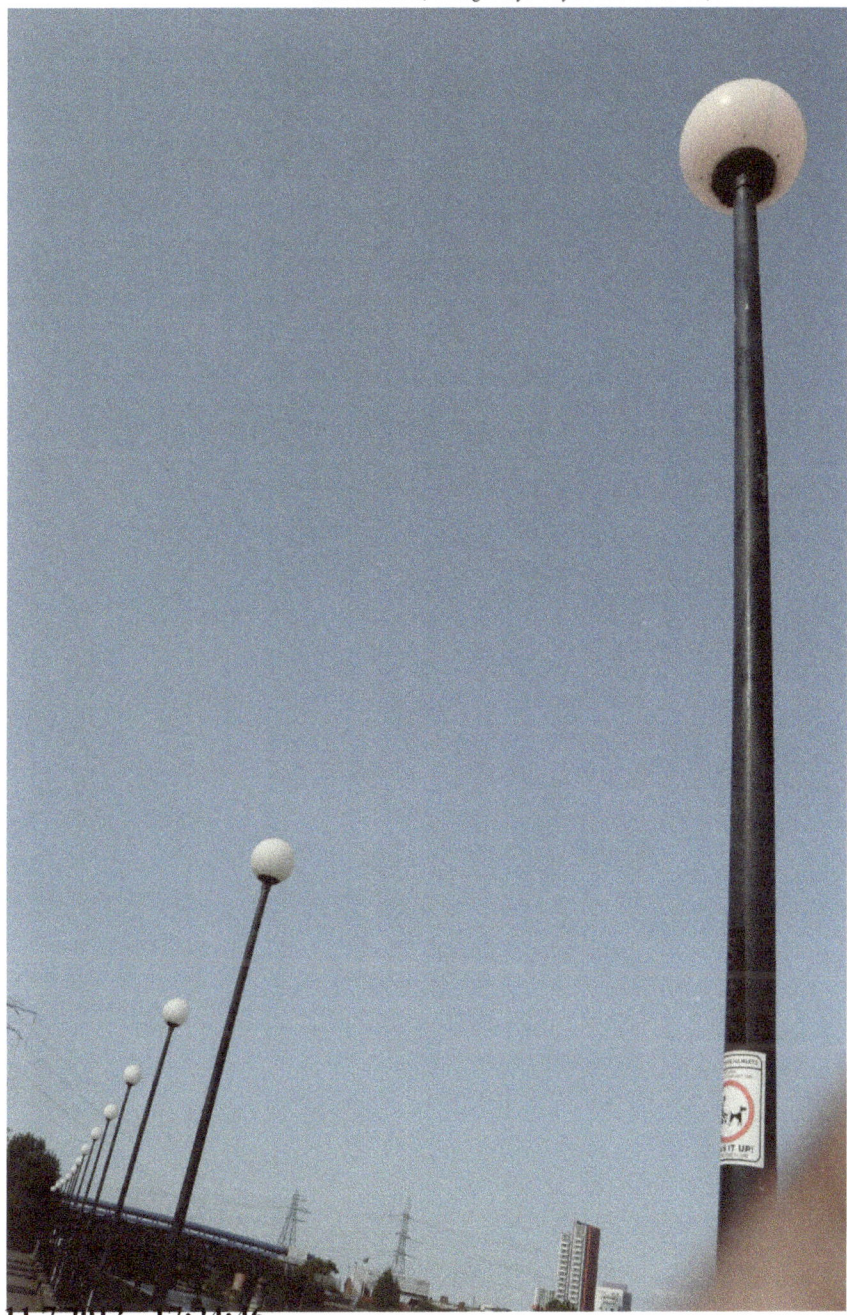

11.7.2013 - 17:24:46

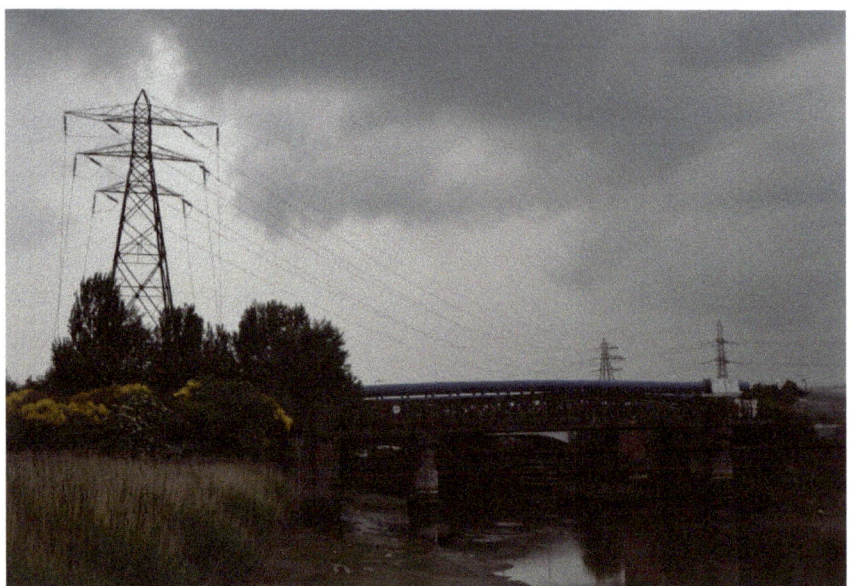

21.6.2013 - 16:45:22

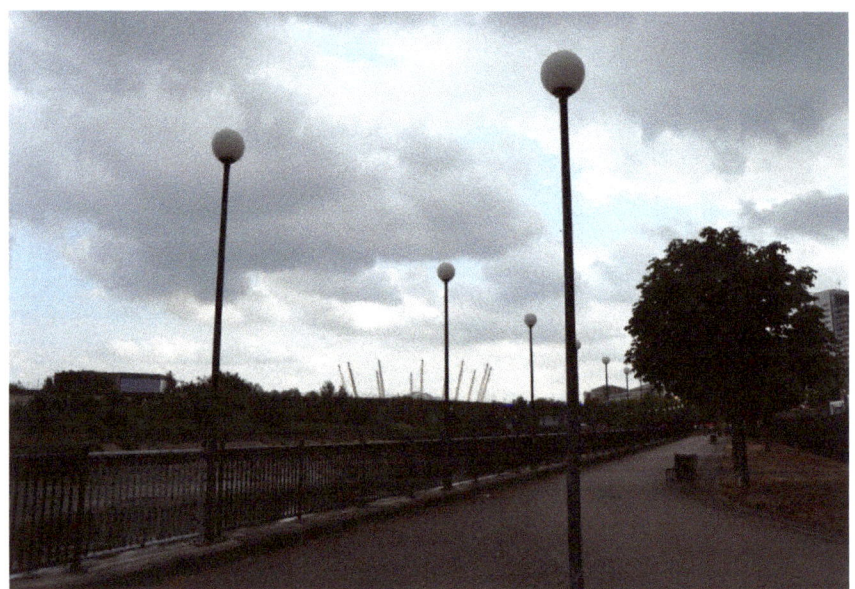

21.6.2013 - 16:45:44

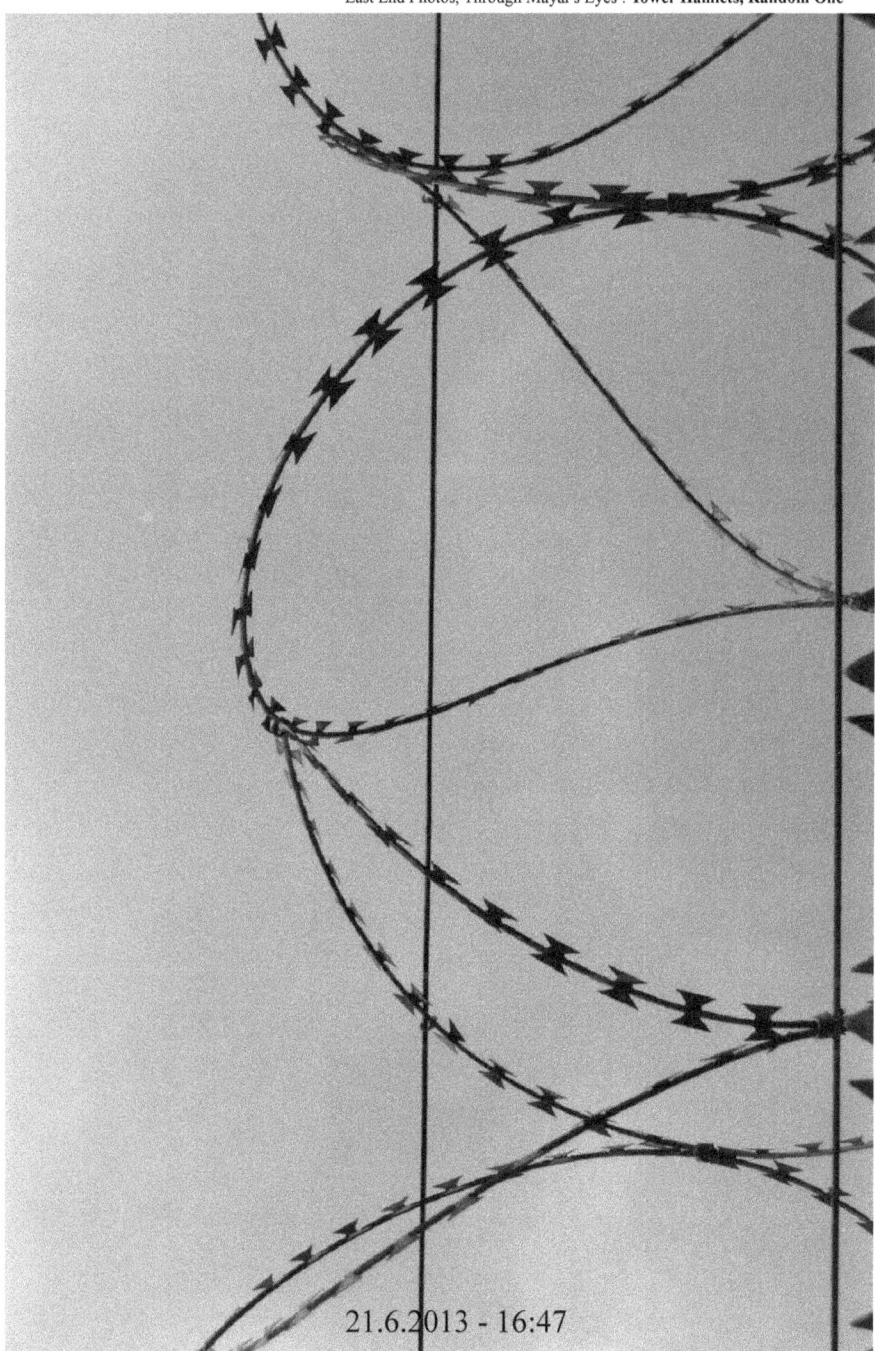

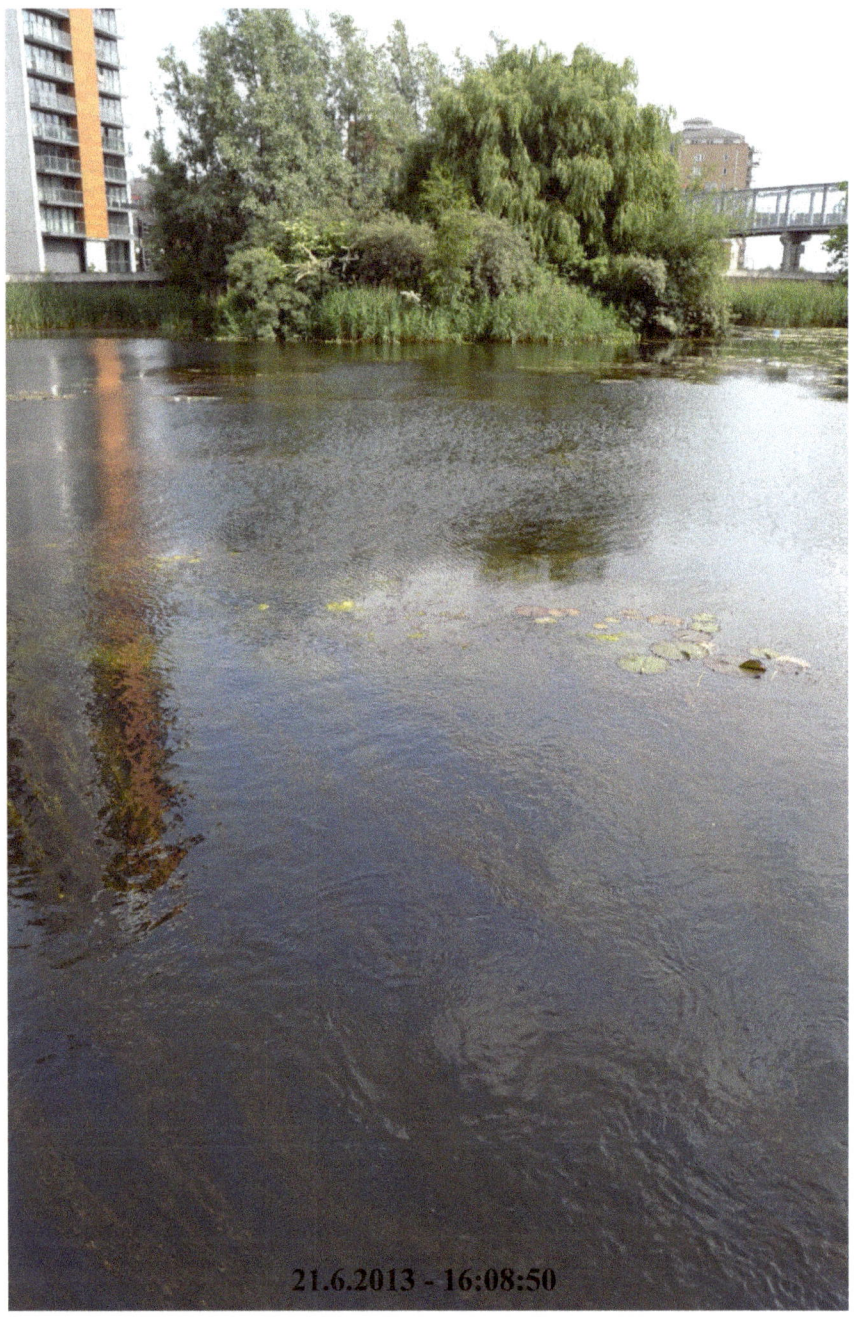

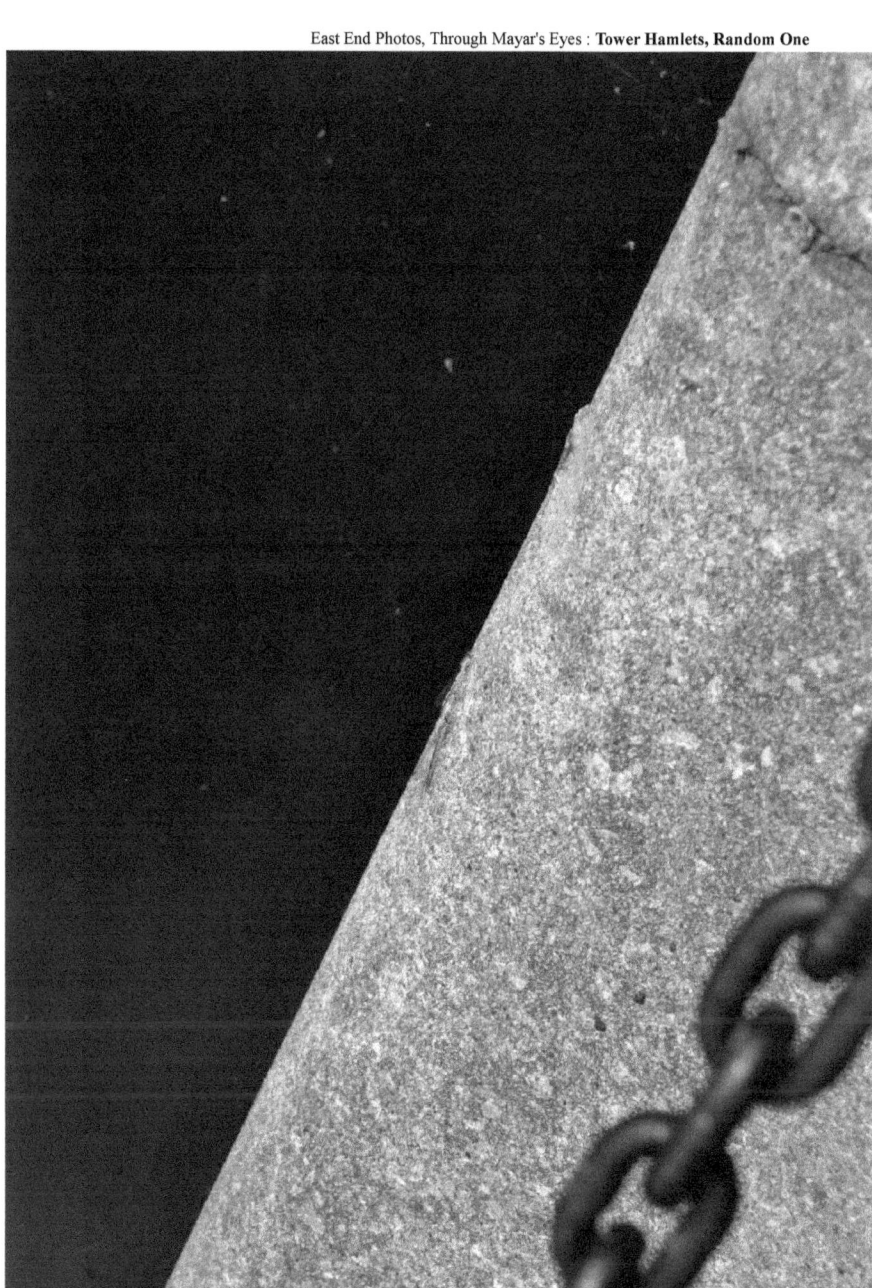

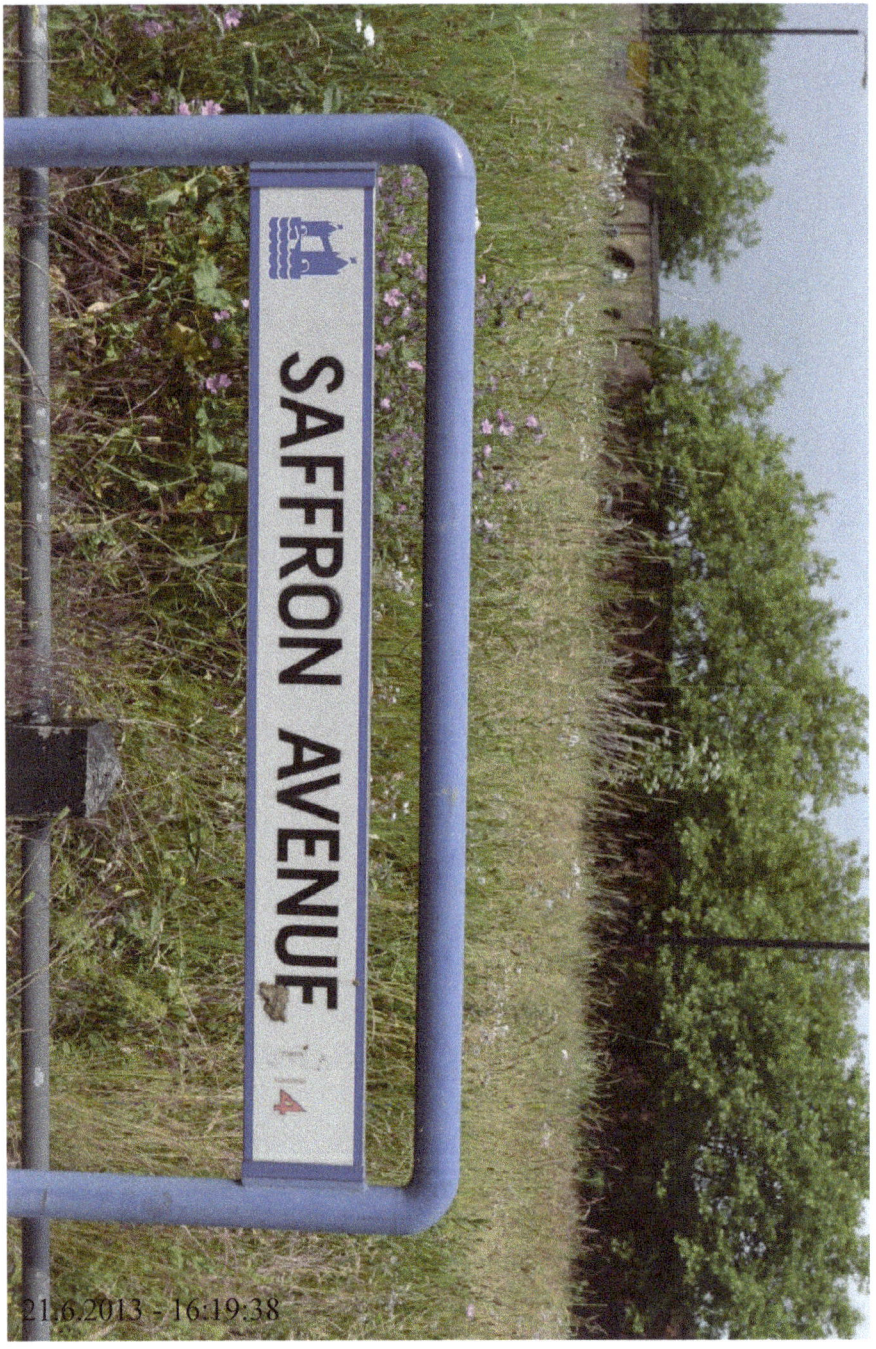

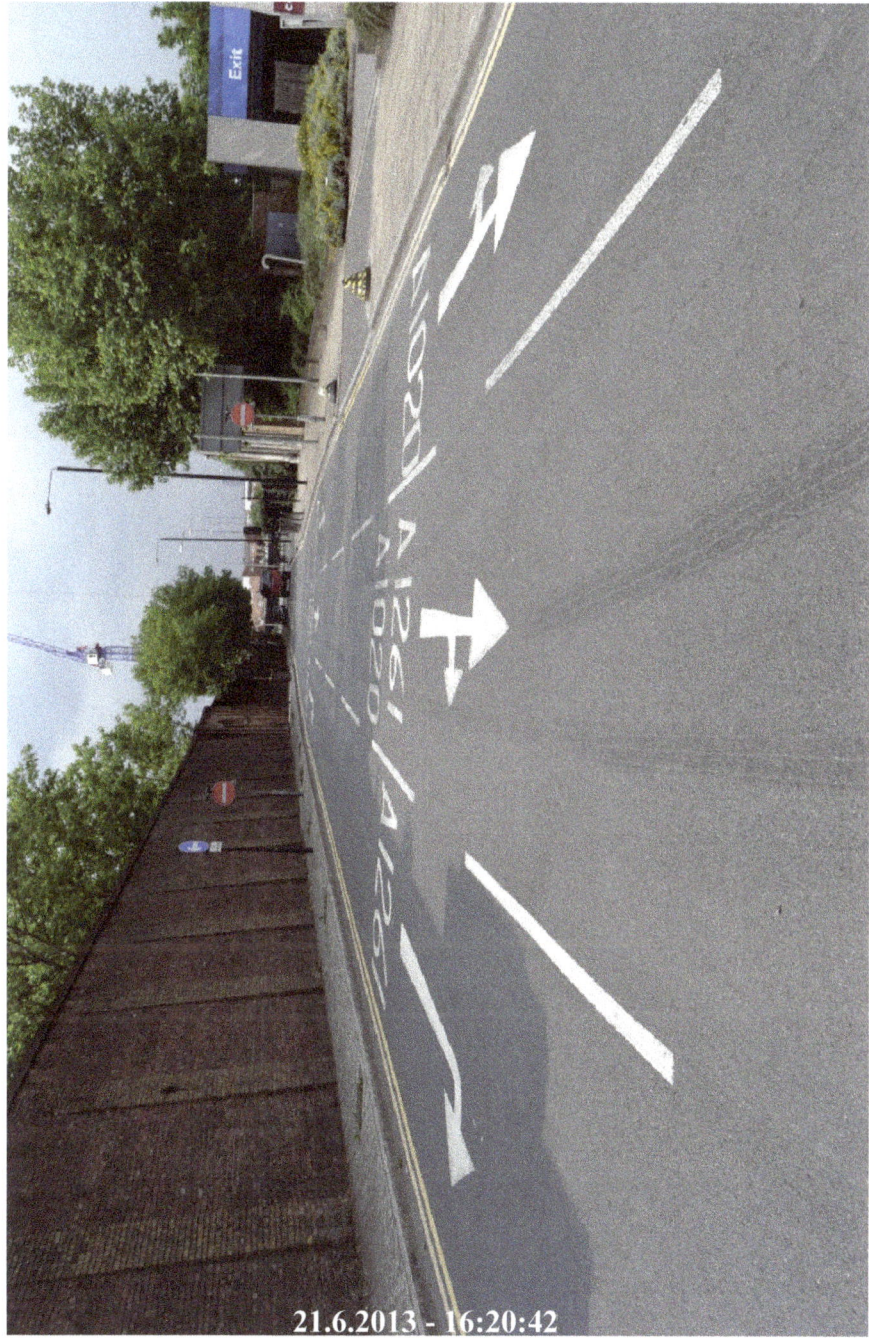

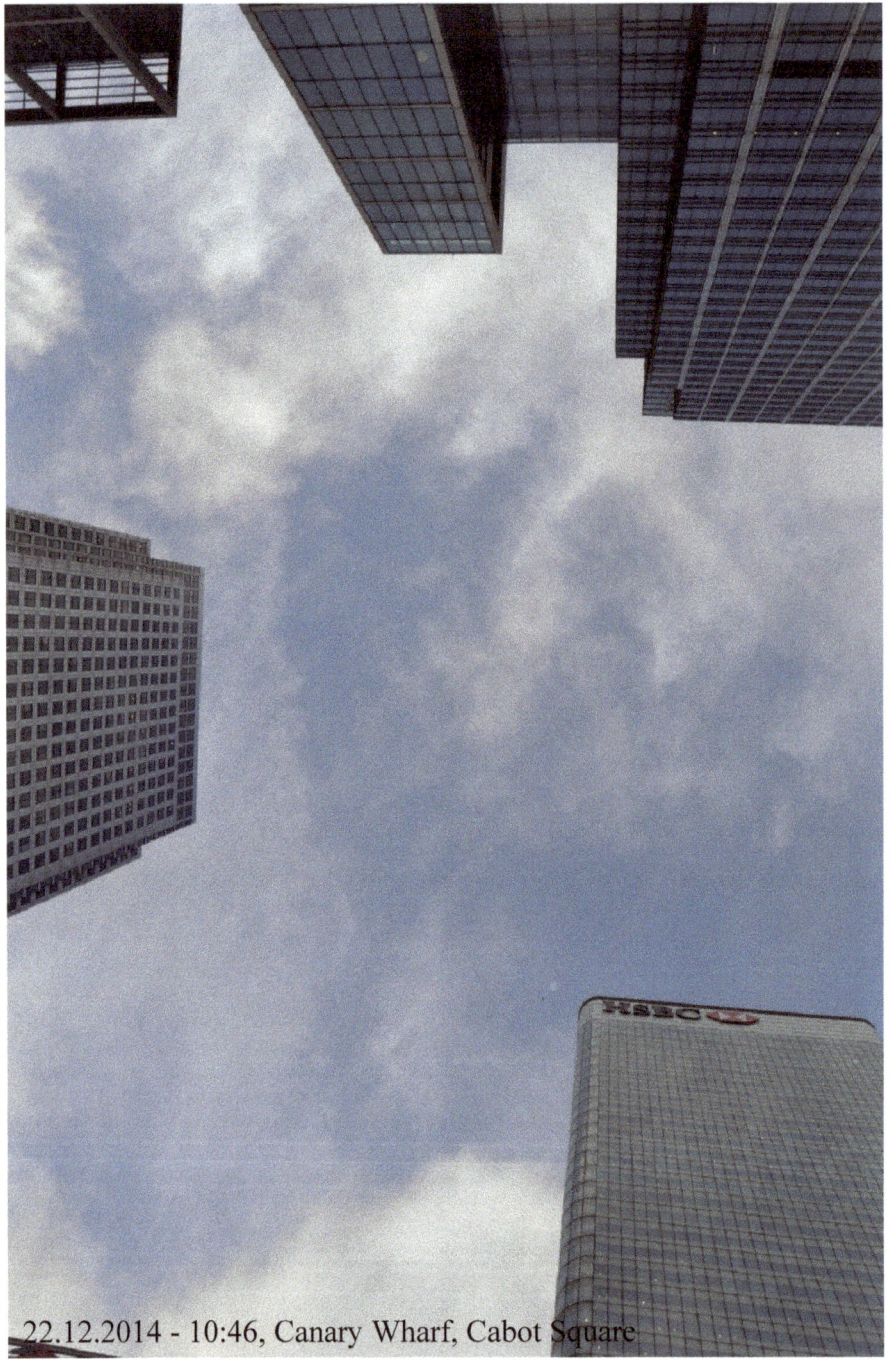

22.12.2014 - 10:46, Canary Wharf, Cabot Square

www.ingramcontent.com/pod-product-compliance
Lightning Source LLC
Chambersburg PA
CBHW040517220526
45473CB00012B/2897